SELF-EMPLOYMENT

Steps to Starting and Growing a Small Business

D1563598

Rick Bean and Bobby Bean

"Self-Employment: Steps to Starting and Growing a Small Business," by Rick Bean. ISBN 978–1–60264–311–6 (soft cover) 978–1-60264–344–4 (ebook).

Published 2009 by Virtualbookworm.com Publishing Inc., P.O. Box 9949, College Station, TX 77842, US. ©2009, Rick Bean. All rights reserved. No part of this publication may be reproduced, stored in a retrieval system, or transmitted in any form or by any means, electronic, mechanical, recording or otherwise, without the prior written permission of Rick Bean.

Manufactured in the United States of America.

HUMBOLDT PARK

This book is dedicated to my cousin and mentor,
Bobby Joe Bean, Jr.

Contents

PREFACE

So why write a book about self-employment when there have been self-employed people, well, as long as there have been people? Why NOW?

Two reasons come to mind. First, anyone who watches the news knows that corporations all across America are right-sizing, down-sizing, outsourcing, merging and in general looking for ways to cut costs. That usually means production workers, supervisors and managers are expendable. Most layoffs affect those at the bottom of a corporation's employment hierarchy. Currently, a lot of "displaced" people are looking for work. In the coming years there will be many more joining the ranks of the unemployed due to corporate cost cutting.

Second, our education system in the United States is good at some things, but encouraging students to seriously consider starting their own businesses right out of high school or college isn't one of them. I want to change that.

As higher paying production jobs and customer service call centers are outsourced to foreign countries, people here at home are faced with replacement jobs in the "service industry."

There's nothing wrong with working in retail, flipping burgers, detailing cars at the local carwash, or many other examples of work in the service sector. Any one of those occupations provides good, honest work. Unfortunately, many of those jobs pay minimum wage. Even in those establishments, were pay is $7 or $8 per hour, try making a mortgage payment, buying fuel, groceries, clothes, paying bills and raising kids on $320 per week ($8 per hour X 40 hours). Of course that reflects gross income. Income taxes and Social Security are withheld

1

before a paycheck is delivered. Take home pay is more like $240 per week.

I know many people who think that $15 per hour is great pay. They are including at least some level of benefits like health insurance and a retirement plan in that calculation. There was a time when that was true. Unfortunately, with inflation eating away at wages and benefits being cut back (almost as fast as I can write this book), reality is that for an individual or a family with a mortgage payment—$15 an hour is, at best, a subsistence wage. Here's the saddest reality of all; most workers in the U.S. don't even come close to $15 per hour, with or without benefits.

I am proof that self-employment is a viable alternative to getting a job. In fact, self-employment is creating your own job. After being employed in a number of different places, I have seen enough to know that there are literally millions of people out there who really dislike what they do or where they do it, and maybe even the people they do it for.

I want to state something right now: I am in NO WAY advocating just quitting a job that is currently paying your bills and providing you with insurance. "Never quit a job until you have something better in hand." That comes straight from my grandfather, who lived through the Depression. I'm sure that was hard earned wisdom for him. He shared it with me—I'm sharing it with you. It's fantastic advice!

However, if you are unhappy with what you're doing, there's no reason you can't start out on weekends or your days off beginning the process of building a side business. Once you start making some money on the side, you'll have a chance to see if what you've chosen to do is enjoyable, profitable and preferable to your current job. I'm willing to bet a day will come where the success you experience in your business and the freedom of working for yourself causes you to decide to go out on your own. There's nothing like working for yourself.

I've come to the conclusion that life is just too short to spend it doing a job I truly dislike or working for a company that I don't respect, or that doesn't respect me. My goal, as I write this, is to help show those who have never considered, or are now considering, making the change from employee to small business owner how to get started and maybe help them avoid some of the mistakes I made along the way. I'm not saying self-employment is easy. It takes a lot of hard work, hustle and flexibility; but, most of all, it takes determination.

If you are still in high school or college, this is the best possible time for you to read this book. You need to know there's absolutely no reason you can't start your own business after leaving school versus working for someone else. If you find yourself laid off, outsourced, right-sized or down-sized and forced into a change, fear not! I started my self-employment journey at the age of 42, in exactly the same circumstances.

I was lucky when I started. I had a mentor, Bobby, my brother, who has been self-employed much of his working life. Much of the advice and many of the strategies in this book came from him to me. Now, I'm sharing them with you. If you don't have a mentor, consider this book, me and Bobby to be yours.

Chapter 1
My Story

GROWING UP AS A kid in America during the 1960s and 70s, I was told to get good grades so I could get a good job. In public schools, the main thrust of education was preparing students to have a job. I think there was an elective course in high school called Entrepreneurial Studies but I didn't take it. If I had my way, there would be a least six classes (two classes in 10th, 11th and 12th grades) on this subject and they would be core requirements for graduating high school. It is a grave disservice to our youth to limit their thinking to "getting a job."

I was a "good" student. Actually, I had a knack for memorizing information, repeating it and being able to eliminate the "wrong" answers on multiple choice tests. As a result, I managed A's and B's from the first grade through high school— with the exceptions of algebra and geometry. Interestingly, I can grasp the applications of geometry on a pool table. Show me an equation on paper and I'm lost. Give me a pool cue and a difficult shot involving angles and ball rotation and my brain is in paradise. Go figure!

I decided during my sophomore year in high school that college wasn't for me. Dad sat me down one day and said he and Mom had talked. If I went to college right after graduating from high school they would find a way to pay for it. My exact words to my dad were "No way! I'm done with school. I'm going to get a job and earn some money!" I'm betting he was disappointed on one hand and a little relieved on the other. College was expensive back then, too. I let my parents off the hook for a substantial financial burden with my decision. Looking back, I wouldn't have made it through college anyway. I wasn't ready to settle down and study.

I ended up graduating high school in Idaho at eighteen and worked in the following occupations: food service, tire re-tread plant, tire warehouse, freight dock, custodial, house construction and, finally, electronics.

My last food service job was in the cafeteria of our local Hewlett-Packard site. I must admit, my interest in getting a job there stemmed more from a long range plan to get hired on with HP than my love for cooking. In our area, getting on full time with HP was like winning the "job lotto." It took three years and two rejections, but in my case the third time really was a charm. I was hired on as a full time employee with HP and for about a year I was walking on air.

Eventually, reality settled in. It's a job. Don't get me wrong, the pay was better than I'd ever had. Back then the benefits package was amazing! As most of us eventually discover, all jobs have irritations and politics. The longer I worked there, the more I came to understand that the vision of Bill Hewlett and David Packard of providing lifetime employment for their workers and the fabled "HP Way" were quickly becoming things of the past.

After ten years at HP, we started hearing rumors that our factory was going to be sold. One day a meeting was called and each shift was pulled into a room and given the news. Yes, it was true. The Formatter Factory (where the printed circuit assemblies that powered HP LaserJet printers were produced) was going to be sold. There was a communal gasp, and immediately after that you could have heard a pin hit the stage. If I've ever experienced a "stunned silence" in my life, it was in that room on that day. We were assured that whoever bought us would keep us all in our jobs.

That turned out to be true. For the next three or four years, the new company kept most of us working. It became obvious, though, that Hewlett Packard's corporate culture and the new owner's were very different. Working under the new company's rules was difficult for long term HP employees.

To make a long, sad story shorter—after eliminating as many poor performers as possible "for cause," the new company offered a VSI (Voluntary Severance Initiative). Bottom line: accept the terms of this severance package and leave now voluntarily, or take your chances on being laid off later with a minimal severance package. To be fair, the VSI was relatively generous—a week's pay for every year of service up to a certain number of years. Frankly, I don't remember what the cap was, but I received over three months' pay. The best thing about the VSI was that if you took it, you still qualified to receive unemployment benefits. I accepted the severance. I then spent 39 weeks on unemployment looking for work.

I was required to apply at two potential employers per week. I'm going to share exactly what my case worker at Job Service told me, in case there are those of you out there in the same circumstances. I asked point blank if I had to accept a $7 per hour job if one was offered. His response was, "Don't apply anywhere you don't want to work." When I asked again, he leaned across the desk and stated emphatically, "Listen to what I'm saying! Don't APPLY anywhere you don't want to WORK." He was trying to communicate something without actually SAYING it. Now I'm going to tell you what I interpreted from that exchange. You are required to APPLY for work—to SEEK work. You are NOT required to FIND work—especially if the work available provides substantially less income than your previous job.

I took his advice and applied for work. Frankly, I applied at places where I knew they weren't hiring but would accept applications. We have a lot of Albertson's grocery stores in my area. I applied at every one of them. In fact, Job Service allows you to update applications after a certain number of weeks and count that toward your weekly seeking requirement. I updated all of my Albertson's applications.

I can already hear some of my readers thinking, "Man! That's just lazy and dishonest. It's like stealing!" I want to share another comment the same case worker at Job Service made to my group of new applicants during the orientation meeting. "Don't feel like accepting unemployment benefits is a hand out. It's not! It's YOUR MONEY! You and your employer paid into the system specifically for a time like this. All you are doing is claiming the benefits you paid in." That revolutionized my thinking about unemployment. I never understood that before. I always looked at it like welfare. It's not. Like the man said, "It's YOUR money."

If you are in a situation where your job is gone and you qualify for unemployment benefits, learn all you can about the rules of the system. Work within those rules, but use them to your advantage. The best thing about having thirty-nine weeks on unemployment is that I was able to decompress. All of us at HP and then the new company had been under huge amounts of stress for five years. Having almost ten months to rest and reevaluate my future, while keeping my bills paid, was priceless!

If you can make it on your unemployment checks, I would advise taking as long as possible to "find" a job. Consider using the time off to begin planning your own business. It's against the rules of unemployment to actually be working a business (earning money) while receiving benefits, but there's nothing in the rules that say you can't be acquiring the equipment, skills and information needed to get started. As long as you are applying at the required number of jobs per week, all is well.

Here's a comment to the folks who administer the Job Service Program. You should revisit this issue. It is ridiculous to tell people those benefits are "their money" on one hand and then tell them they can't use the time and money to start up a self-employment venture on the other. The country would be much better served if tens of thousands of those people went out during the benefits period and started small businesses without fear of being penalized. Look, if they say that's what they're doing and blow the money, too bad for them. They wasted "their money." They only have a limited amount available to them. At that point their only recourse will be to accept an entry level job. If they are successful, however, they will eventually be paying into the system again and may even create jobs for other unemployed persons thus making the job of finding work for the unemployed easier.

I was very frustrated at the roadblocks I encountered in the system. It makes no sense to require those receiving benefits to use the benefits ONLY to get a job working for someone else. That's my opinion.

During my stint on unemployment, I took a series of aptitude tests at Job Service for continuing education. My counselor selected a number of occupations for me to look at based on the results of those tests. They ranged from dental assistant to tile setter. There was information about each occupation, like current job availability, projected growth of each industry and salary range. The thing that struck me most out of all the data was that the highest salary I could expect was $15.65 an hour, as a tile setter, and that was after working four years as an apprentice.

I called Bobby and was complaining about the top pay for the tile job being $15.65 per hour after four years, he listened patiently and let me vent, then he said, "Do you still remember what I showed you about washing windows?"

He had done that years before and I'd never really used the skills so I said, "Well, uh yeah—kind of—I guess."

Bobby said, "Look, instead of working for someone else why don't you start a window cleaning business and work for yourself?"

Those words and many more that followed changed how I look at work. Actually, they changed my life.

Chapter 2
My Mentor—Bobby

BOBBY STARTED WORKING FOR himself in high school mowing lawns to earn money for his first car. At age twenty-two, he started a swimming pool maintenance business. Then, for a few years, he worked as a waiter at a nice restaurant. At twenty-seven, Bobby became truly self-employed as a full time window cleaner. For 3 years, that was his primary focus. At age thirty, he decided he wanted to be able to move around and still have the ability to earn good money wherever he lived. His next venture (in addition to window cleaning) was to become certified as a hair stylist.

Right out of school, Bobby tried to work in a high end salon. That experience didn't go so well, so after about a year he made a change. He applied for a position as manager in a department store hair salon and was hired. He spent a year constantly cutting hair and perfecting the skills he'd learned at school. While there, he also learned to manage a business, order and inventory supplies, keep books and manage people. Bobby's statement about the year he spent there was, "Taking that job was the best thing I ever did! It taught me how to run a business." The year he spent there is a good example of serving an apprenticeship. There will be more on apprenticeships in a later chapter.

After that year, he rented a chair in a private salon again. This time he was ready. He continued washing windows as well as styling hair. Over a ten year period Bobby moved around the Pacific Northwest and out to Maui, Hawaii a number of times. His longest stay was on Maui for about 5 years. I'm happy that was the case because I was able to visit him there three times. The third time, I got to spend 3 months helping in a condo cleaning business while the owner recovered from surgery. A three month working vacation on Maui was a once-in-a-lifetime experience for me.

Now he's back in the Pacific Northwest and has added a realtor's license to his hair styling certification and is practicing in both occupations.

Why did I spend so much time telling you about myself and Bobby? I want you to know that neither one of us has a four year college degree. Our parents aren't wealthy. We're not geniuses. We're just plain guys who learned how to be self-employed and make a living by creating our own jobs. If you follow the basic steps outlined in the rest of the book, you can too.

Chapter 3
Why Self-Employment?

I DECIDED TO GO into self-employment out of necessity. None of the jobs available during the recession, that ended my electronics "career," paid anywhere near enough to cover my mortgage payment and allow me to eat.

Bobby wanted the freedom to move around, see different places and still make a good living. Self-employment allowed him to do that.

My friend, Gary, wanted to get out of his office job and work from home.

Let me ask you a question. Have you ever heard someone you know say, "I hate my job" or "I'm really tired of my boss" or "This employer could care less about me"? As far as you could tell, did they mean it? A lot of people grouse about work conditions but really aren't that unhappy. Some really DO hate their job. Every person you've ever heard say something like that, who is self-motivated and reliable is a candidate to run their own small business.

Life is too short to spend it working in a job or industry that makes you miserable. There's no amount of money, no benefits package, and certainly no veneer of "security" that's worth spending one third of your life in a place that literally makes you crazy. As for the security issue, if you've been watching the news over the last ten years, you can't possibly have missed all the layoffs and outsourcing that's been going on. If you are like me, you've experienced it for yourself. Even if you haven't, I bet you know someone who has.

As I started out, one of Bobby's first sayings to me was, "A self-employed person is a self-starter." Every phone call, he would say that again and again. Why? Simply put, it is the underlying truth of self-employment. No one will care about your business like you will. Self-employed people should be waking up every day and asking, "What's on the schedule for today?" If the answer is "nothing," you should be asking, "Where am I going to advertise today?" Another question you should be constantly asking yourself is, "How can I improve my business or businesses today?"

You will find that once you start building your first business, one of Bobby's observations will happen, you will start looking around at everything you see and asking, "Can I make a business out of that and what would it take to do it?"

Once you start working, you will make your first $20 per hour on a job and think, "I can't believe it! I made $20 per hour." Then, as you get more efficient at what you do, you will find your dollars per hour will climb. You will make $25 per hour for the same work, then $30 per hour. You won't have to raise your rate, you'll just get the job done more efficiently. The key here is to charge by the job, not by the hour. If you tell a potential client you charge $35 per hour for work, many won't hire you. If you tell them you will do the job for $100 and they agree, you know you can get done in 3 hours tops, you have just made $33.33 per hour for the same work.

Here's another thing Bobby told me would happen. He said, "You will get to a point where you are making a living with your physical labor work. Then, you'll start asking yourself what you can make a business out of that will require less physical labor and at the same time earn you more money." He was absolutely right. That's exactly how it's gone for me. I still wash windows. I have a lawn mowing service. I do hauling if a client needs that done since I have a truck and trailer. I started a retail business selling knives on weekends. Many of my customers asked if I sharpened knives, so I purchased a sharpening machine and have learned how to sharpen knives and scissors as well. Now I'm writing a book.

Self-employment is a mindset. If you've always worked a job for someone else who directed your work effort, you will need to adjust that thinking. As you read this book, start contemplating that. I had to make that transition. You can make it as well.

I'm going to focus a few paragraphs on a phenomenon that I can almost guarantee will happen. Any time someone decides to do something different, than either they or others in their family have done before, they will run into *naysayers*. These will be, for the most part, well-meaning people who will say things like, "It'll never work!" or "You don't know anything about running a business!" or "No one in our family has ever been self-employed." You will hear general statements that it's too risky, no one will hire you, or more to the point—some will just tell you that you will fail.

When you encounter this (and you probably will—I did), you will be told the safest thing you can do is to get another job. Naysayers have a tendency to project their own fears onto those they are giving the advice.

Here's the bottom line. What's the worst thing that can happen if you try to start your own small service business and after six months or a year you just aren't making it? You go get a job, right? Remember, there's nothing wrong with finding a part time job that has fixed hours to provide a steady check and ALSO starting a small business.

I love my Mom. When I told her I had decided to take the VSI and leave the electronics industry, she suggested I should reconsider and take any job the company offered me. I decided to take the VSI. A little over a year after I left, the factory closed down. All the people who had scrambled around and landed a job with the company ended up unemployed anyway. In the meantime, I'd had a year of rest, and finally had a clear mind about where I was going and what I was going to do—-self-employment.

I realized after a year of window cleaning full time that I was going to need another business. It would have required years to build a clientele large enough to provide a living. In most cases people only use a window cleaner once or twice a year. I would have needed at least 400 clients to earn a living.

I looked around and saw hundreds of guys with pickup trucks and trailers driving around and mowing lawns. I figured I could mow a lawn as well as anyone else and added it to my list of services provided. For one person to make a living in an area where mowing is seasonal requires about 30 clients.

After three years of watching me build my businesses, my Mom told me I'd made the right decision by going out on my own. Something that has always interested me about human nature is that my mom herself had been "right-sized" out of a couple of banking jobs right before she retired, and still, her advice was for me to take another job. I'm not faulting my mom. She was advocating taking the "safe" road. People are inclined to go with what they know.

What I've learned about working for myself is how much money employers make off of their employees' efforts. The best job I ever had, paid less than $15 per hour (plus benefits). I've made as much as $50 per hour on selected window cleaning jobs. I average $30, or better, per hour in most things I do.

In the end, listening to naysayers limits you. You are giving your hopes and dreams over to those who have never had the creativity, courage or initiative to pursue their own. If your dream is to have your own small business, research your chosen field, talk to people who are currently doing it and ask for advice—then go for it!

Another one of Bobby's sayings, and this is a great place for it, "Dream big, start small. Start big, make big mistakes—start small, make small mistakes." This has proven true in my efforts. By starting small, I learned the hard lessons at a small price. As you learn and continue advertising, your business will grow and so will your experience base. Millions of people are self-employed. If you are willing to work hard and are self-motivated you can be successful in your own business. Someday, if you are willing to manage people, you can become an employer and reap the rewards of having people work for you. You will have a much better chance of becoming financially independent as an employer than you ever will as an employee.

Be sure to give the respect due to family and friends, but make your own decisions. Base those decisions on the best planning and research you can do, but choose the path that makes the most sense for YOU. Those naysayers aren't going to be grinding away in that factory or store or restaurant. YOU are.

I wouldn't have had the success I've experienced without Bobby as a mentor. If you have someone in your family that is self-employed, or friends or acquaintances who have their own businesses, go to them and ask them for advice. Ask them how they got started. Ask them to share with you the best decisions and worst decisions they made starting out. Ask them to help you with ideas. Finally, ask them if you can call them occasionally as you move forward if you have questions. Do NOT ask them for money.

If you don't have anyone like that—read and reread this book.

Chapter 4
Write It Down!

I'M GOING TO DEVOTE a small chapter to this important concept. If you are thinking about a self-employment opportunity, sit down with pen and paper and write it down. If you do this on your computer, print it out once it's completed. This is important because as long as you're just thinking about it, it's only an idea. As you start writing, you take it from the realm of idea or dream and give it life. Once you have it on paper you can hold it, look at it and show it to others. Writing it down makes it real.

Start out with the general concept. Write a paragraph or two (or a page or two if you want) describing the business you want to run. Once you have that, start thinking about what you will need to make the concept into a business. What equipment or tools will you need? What products? How will you advertise? What type of vehicle is most suited to your business?

If you don't already know how much your monthly bills are, I'm betting you don't have a monthly budget written down. Now is an excellent time to make one. Include all your monthly payments like groceries, fuel, rent/mortgage, power, natural gas, water/sewer/trash, car payment, credit cards, doctor bills—you get the idea. Don't forget things like insurance premiums that are every 6 months. Also, if you will record small expenses like lattes, fast food and convenience store stops for a couple of months, you will be amazed at how much money is spent this way. Hundreds of dollars per month! Millions of Americans go to work, earn money and pay bills without a clear idea of how much they spend, simply because they don't have a budget. As a person who runs your own business, you will need to know exactly what you spend each month and what that expense is for.

If you decide to start the business, there's another written document that also makes the business real—not only to you, but to potential clients. In fact, it's probably the most important advertising item any self-employed business person can have. You need to design a business card. I recommend a basic black letter on white card stock for your first one. Any printing shop can make these for you inexpensively. Shop around because prices do vary. Some of the "big box" office supply stores offer truly inexpensive business cards. You'll get the best rate by purchasing at least 1,000 at a time.

Bobby told me business cards would make my business real. I whined about spending $70 on the first thousand. When I opened that box of cards and pulled one out and looked at it, what he told me was right on. I was a business owner. The card made it real. I actually got choked up looking at that card. Don't be surprised if you do too.

Finally, once you start your business and have clients, you need to have a billing system that is professional. This means using either a computer generated invoice or a duplicate invoice book which can be purchased at any office supply store. Invoices scribbled on scraps of paper are unprofessional. Clients appreciate receiving a professional looking invoice.

To sum it up: writing out your dream makes it real. Putting that writing into practice creates your business. Professionally printed business cards make your business real to others.

Chapter 5
Help! I Need Work Now!

OKAY. YOU'VE BEEN FIRED, laid off, right-sized, downsized or merged out of work and your job is now being done by someone in another country for a tenth of the pay. Welcome to outsourcing! If you are anything like me, you are (or were) angry and feeling betrayed by your former employer. Anger and frustration are normal responses to having <u>financial security</u> yanked out from under you. So is shock. This is especially true if you've given many years of hard work and made personal sacrifices that benefited your former employer.

While these are normal feelings, they are counter-productive to moving forward. As you read on, consider putting that emotional energy into building your own business.

Probably the fastest way to start making money is to provide a service. There are two main reasons. <u>Basic service</u> skills are quick and easy to learn and start-up costs are minimal. A list, that is by no means comprehensive, would include: lawn mowing, window cleaning (wonder why those two top my list?), house cleaning, pressure washing, hauling, construction cleanup, bush trimming, tree trimming, <u>child care</u> provider, handyman, computer setup and repair, general electronics repair, mechanical repair, <u>auto repair</u>, and so on. I mean, anything you know how to do that other people either can't, won't or don't want to do can be offered as a service.

Here's an offbeat example I saw on a television show—a pooper-scooper service. No joke! A lady had built up a business (a very profitable one) contracting with dog owners, to show up once or twice a week, and clean up after their dogs. If you like dogs and want a low cost business idea, this is it. You need a reliable vehicle, a plastic bucket, small trash can liners that fit in the bucket and a long handled scooper.

After you finish laughing, consider this. If you built up a clientele of 20 people who used your service and paid you $15 (more if they have multiple dogs) for two visits each week—and each stop took approximately 15 minutes, you'd be making $1,200 per month. Really! You are earning $300 per week for about 10 hours work plus travel time. That's $30 per hour to clean up after dogs. Now, stretch your imagination, say you double your clientele, all of a sudden you are working, maybe, 25 hours per week (including travel time) and earning at least $600. You're working outside with dogs (assuming you are a dog person) and you are working for yourself, and did I mention you are making $600 per week?!?

My point here is that any self-motivated person can start a small business and offer a basic service to people and build up a clientele willing to pay them for the service. Are you a self-motivated person? You can do this.

I mow lawns. With 25 clients, I currently work about 25 hours per week at that business and earn in excess of $3,000 per month. That's part time. I'm able to do that about 7 months out of the year here in Idaho.

I helped a friend, a single mom, start a house cleaning business. The tools needed were basic cleaning supplies available at most stores, a caddy to carry them around the house, a vacuum cleaner and a reliable car. Within a year she had enough income from her client base to pay rent, meet her bills and probably most importantly to her—have the flexibility to get her kids to and from school without worrying about losing a job. She just explained her kid's school schedule to her clients and they worked with her around that schedule. Most clients will work with you if you ask.

If you need income now, ask yourself, "What do I know how to do that people will pay me to do for them?" Next question, "Do I have the necessary equipment on hand right now to do that or can I get it free or inexpensively?" The most fundamental equipment a self-employed person MUST have is reliable transportation. Why? Reliability. I've picked up a lot of jobs because the prior service provider was unreliable. Having a vehicle that conks out periodically contributes to being labeled unreliable by clients. In a service business, being dependable will keep you working and your clients happy.

If at all possible, select either a small 4-cylinder pickup or a minivan. Either one will allow you to carry your work equipment and probably allow you to haul a small trailer, if necessary. Also, a 4-cylinder will save you a lot of money in fuel expenses.

Once you have reliable transportation, a service to provide and the equipment needed to provide it, resist the impulse to run out and immediately start looking for paying clients. I recommend practicing your service on your own house or property first. If you don't have a house, go to family and friends and explain that you are starting your own service business. Offer to provide your service to them for free so you can practice. If they offer to pay you anyway, gratefully accept the money. Also, ask them to give you honest feedback about your work and to offer suggestions for improvements you can make. Now is not the time to have thin skin. You are going to be working for strangers and you want to offer the best service possible. Minor criticisms from family and friends will hurt you a lot less than being fired by a paying client. You don't need to be an expert at what you do, but you need to achieve a basic level of proficiency before charging people money for your services.

I am not the world's best lawn mower or window cleaner. I know I'm not the fastest. Yet I have a loyal group of people who hire me every year to clean their windows and mow their lawns. Why? I try to keep my prices reasonable and above all, I do everything I can to be dependable!

Please engrave those last two words in your mind—BE DEPENDABLE! Number one: have reliable transportation— number two: be dependable.

If you are scheduled to be somewhere, be there on time or make a point of calling the client and letting them know you'll be late. If something comes up and you just can't make it there, call, tell them why and be truthful. Most clients will be so happy you called, they will reschedule without any problem.

Here's a real life situation from my window cleaning business. I'm a little old-school and use a paper calendar to schedule window cleaning jobs. My client called and left a polite voice mail that said, "I thought we had an appointment for today, but maybe I was mistaken. Please call me as soon as you get this message. Thank you." I called as soon as I heard the voice mail. I realized I'd written the job down and it was still on the table—not on the calendar. I apologized profusely and explained what I'd done and asked what day she would like to reschedule and made sure her job was the first of that day. She was very gracious and understanding. In my experience, most clients will give you the benefit of the doubt if you establish a pattern of being honest and forthright with them.

Having good client relationship skills is essential. It is vital to develop the ability of speak with clients in a clear, direct and professional manner. You are the CEO (Chief Executive Officer) of your business and you need to present a friendly and professional face to your clients and potential clients. Smile a lot and be ready to give them a firm handshake at all times. Care about your clients. You don't have to be friends, but it's nice if you are. Having a good rapport with your clients makes the working relationship much smoother. Treat them and their property with the same respect you treat yourself and your property (or better). The Golden Rule strikes again!

Another story from my past; the first day I started advertising my window cleaning business, I was hanging fliers on doors in my neighborhood. I didn't speak with anyone, just hung the flyer and moved on. At one of the houses there was a lady watering her flowers out front. All I had to say was, "May I give you a flier about my window cleaning business?" I was petrified! It was all I could do to stutter out the sentence about the flier. She was very nice and took it. I practically ran away from her. I realized right then that if I was going to work for people I had to get over being afraid of speaking with them. If you have a fear of speaking with strangers, you are NOT alone. I overcame that fear. You can overcome it as well. You'll have to in order to be self-employed.

Finally, the third most important piece of equipment every small business owner must have is a cell phone. If you don't have one, get one! The phone and monthly service fees are tax write-offs. You need to be able to contact clients (or have them contact you) easily. With the variety and low cost of phones and service plans, there's no excuse for not having one. I resisted getting one for years. I always said, "The only way I'll ever have a cell phone is if I'm making my living using it." Now, I am.

Another area Bobby recently corrected me on was not having voice mail programmed into the cell phone. He pointed out that I should be checking my phone messages after each job. If I only have access to messages at home, I have to wait until I get home at the end of the day to check them. If people can leave a message on my cell phone, I can check them immediately. Good advice from my mentor. I have since corrected that and clients can now leave messages at both phone numbers. Losing even one lawn mowing job because the potential client couldn't get hold of me and in the meantime called someone else could cost me between $750 and $1,500 per year.

Chapter 6
Advertising

THIS CHAPTER IS THE nuts and bolts of how to get started advertising. If you're tired of reading put the book down and rest. You'll need to focus on this chapter. Advertising is the key to self-employment. Getting potential clients to call you concerning your business is what it's all about.

You've written down your idea, listed the equipment and materials needed to do your business, gone out and acquired them, created a budget so you know how much money you need to earn every month to pay your bills and now you need clients.

The first place to look is those people closest to you. In this order—family, friends and then acquaintances, like former co-workers, and if you are comfortable with it, at church or other places where you know a number of people. Let all these people know what you are doing and that you are looking for clients. Offer to work for them at a discounted rate once or twice to show the quality of your work so they'll have confidence in referring you to others.

Bobby has some wisdom about advertising: "Don't be a secret agent. Tell everyone you know or that you meet, who you are and what you are doing."

"You are what you SAY you are." If you tell a potential client that you are a hair stylist, they will take that at face value and probably ask things like, "Oh, where do you work?" or "How long have you been doing that?" People will almost always accept what you say. If you believe you can do what you advertise to others, so will they.

Once you have spoken with family, friends and acquaintances, it's time to get started. You didn't think you were done, did you? Not even close!

I'm going to introduce you to the most economical and physically beneficial method of advertising you can do—door to door. You need to break *inertia*. Inertia is defined as an object at rest. If you are sitting on your couch, you won't ever build a business. You've got to get up and MOVE. The best way to do that is walking fliers door to door.

I can hear you groaning. I know you are because I did when Bobby told me that's what I needed to do. After he convinced me to get started, (I'll admit I didn't try very hard at first), he called and asked if I had any work yet. I told him, "No, I haven't had any calls." He asked if I had passed out fliers that day. My reply, "Well, no." He asked, "Why not?"

What he said next was, "Look, stop feeling sorry for yourself. Get off your backside and walk fliers. When we hang up, get ready, take at least 50 fliers and get to work! That's right, I said WORK! You have to look at distributing your fliers like it's your JOB! You do it every day, whether you want to or not. Even if you aren't getting paid to walk fliers you are making an investment in your business. If you do it, I promise you that a day will come, SOON, where you are so busy working and earning money, you won't have time to walk fliers."

I basically told him I didn't believe that. He said, "Listen, trust me here. It'll happen. I'm going to call you every day for the next couple of weeks and make sure you are walking fliers." He did and I distributed fliers every day.

Within three months, I had so many calls for window cleaning that I was too busy to walk fliers on a daily basis. Of course, Bobby knew this would happen because he'd gone through this process a number of times himself.

You need to realize that walking fliers door to door is a numbers game. Realistically, you can expect a 1 percent return on your effort. It doesn't sound that great until you really look at it. Your business cards or fliers cost between 3-7 cents each. Every hundred you distribute costs you between $3 and $7. If you get one job for each hundred, you will easily pay for the cards and the fuel needed to drive where you distributed them. If the business you've chosen is one that you do on a regular basis, like house cleaning or lawn maintenance, one client could equate to $1,000 per year or more. All for a 3 to 7 cent piece of paper and the time invested in walking it to potential clients. It's hard to beat that for economic efficiency.

Another great reason to advertise this way is the exercise factor. You'll be amazed at how good you feel, physically, after walking cards for 45 minutes or so every day. You may feel stiff after the first few days, but if you've been sedentary for awhile that's to be expected. Spend a few minutes stretching before you head out. Also, leave the dress shoes at home and wear a comfortable pair of tennis shoes or hiking boots. Gel inserts for your shoes are a great investment if you are going to walk fliers.

Bobby is a great believer in fliers. He designs them so that he can get two fliers from one 81/2 X 11 sheet of paper. Once he has a flier designed, he will go to a local printer and have a thousand of them printed up and cut in half for him—instant supply of 2,000 fliers. He staples a rubber band on the corner of each flier for ease of hanging on door and screen handles, and then distributes thirty per day. That's his method. Of course, he's also working each day as well.

Fliers are better if you are in a business where there is a lot of detail you want to convey to potential clients. Bobby is a hair stylist and offers a lot of different salon services. A flyer allows him to create a short biography about himself—for example, how long he's been a stylist, the color line he uses, a list of the services he provides and perhaps a special offer for responding to the flier. A good thing to add on your flier is a special offer to clients for referring someone to your business, maybe a small discount on future service.

If you aren't working, start out with thirty per day until you get in better shape, then gradually increase the number of fliers you put out each day. I personally shoot for 100 per day. If you do that faithfully five days a week for one month, you'll have about 2,200 fliers distributed.

I prefer to use business cards as my advertisement. I use a heavy duty (2-hole) punch and place a hole in the center of one end of the card. You can purchase these punches at any office supply store for about $10, and will punch 5–10 cards at one time. Then, I take a #18 rubber band, also available at most office supply stores, and loop it through the hole in each card for an instant compact door hanging advertisement. Before the card is printed, show the printer where you are going to punch the hole, so no lettering will be damaged, you want your business card to look as professional as possible. Don't forget that business cards can have printing on both sides. On the back in a smaller font, you can include information about your pricing, business policies, work area, services available, etc.

Lawn mowing is a good example of a business where a card hung on someone's door is sufficient. I like business cards because they are small and easy to carry. Most people know what is involved in lawn mowing and if they are in the market for that service, they will call you for a bid. You can use a flier if you prefer.

One thing I can tell you about hanging business cards on doors is that people save them. I've had people call me 2 years after I advertised in their subdivision and ask me to come out and give them an estimate. When I asked how they heard about me, they pulled the card (with the rubber band still attached) from a drawer. This has happened at least three times.

Walking fliers or cards is a great way to get motivated and get out there! Another benefit is, as you walk around you will become familiar with the different street names in subdivisions. When people call you to come give them a bid, you will have a basic idea of where they live.

If you can possibly afford it, especially if you need work ASAP, get some people to help you walk your advertisements. It's worth paying someone $8 to $10 per hour to double or triple your daily advertising output. The sooner you've distributed one thousand fliers, the sooner you can expect that 1 percent return of ten or more calls. Having people help you will get the work done faster and you can write off what you pay them as a business expense on your taxes if you choose. It's a good idea to hire people you trust. I would suggest always going out as a team. There is safety in numbers. Also, decide specifically how you want this done and explain this to your helpers in detail before starting out.

I have a personal philosophy about how I do door to door solicitation. It's based on my observations of people soliciting in my neighborhood and on my own personal likes and dislikes. Your method should reflect yours.

In a nutshell:
1. Never knock or ring a door bell to solicit. I leave the ad and move on.
2. Never leave an ad at a residence where there is a NO SOLICITING sign.
3. Never walk across people's lawns. Only use driveways and walkways.
4. Never step on hoses, toys, etc. Treat people's property with respect.
5. Never "hard sell" when homeowners are outside. Offer your card, thank them for their time and move on.

If you are using helpers, make sure they understand YOUR way of doing this and that they are to do it your way. You and your helpers represent your business. You want to leave a positive impression even before you meet a potential client. You might be surprised at how many people watch when strangers walk up to their homes. I can't tell you how many times I've left a card on a door and before I got back to the street the door opened and a hand reached out to remove the card. I've never liked having solicitors walk across my lawn. I think it's rude and shows a lack of respect. Most of all, show respect to people and their property.

Another method of advertising is magnetic signs on your vehicle. The beauty of these is that you spend about $100 once, and you get years of advertising out of that investment. I recommend a magnetic sign for each side of your vehicle and one for the back. I've seen hundreds of self employed people place magnetic advertisements on the sides of their vehicle and miss the opportunity of having a captive audience for their ad at the back of the vehicle at each and every stop sign and stop light. For that minute, the people behind you have little to do but read your sign. If you've ever watched people waiting at a light, you've seen them reading people's magnetic ads. In fact, I've had people call me from their car sitting next to me or behind me in traffic to set up an appointment for a bid because they read my sign. Magnetic signs work!

Depending on the rules where you live, another advertising opportunity is a simple sign in your front yard. Some places don't allow this, but unless it's specifically prohibited in residential covenants, it can be a very effective method of obtaining work in your local area. Don't pass up any reasonable method of getting the word out about your business/businesses.

Direct mailing can be an effective method of advertising. There are companies who send those envelopes to your house that are stuffed full of different advertisements. If you have a large advertising budget, this can be one method to use. Typically, mass mailings like this cost hundreds to thousands of dollars each time you do it.

If you run a business or service that targets small businesses, you can do direct mailing yourself. Use the phone book and a local Chamber of Commerce membership list to find businesses that use your products or services. Type a short cover letter about yourself and your products and include a business card. If you go to the physical location of many of these businesses, you will find a NO SOLICITING sign on their door. Direct mailing your letter and business card accomplishes two things. It gets past that sign and shows initiative to potential clients. This can make the difference to some business owners. Bear in mind, many of them started out just like you; providing a service. They know how much work goes into preparing and distributing personalized advertisements. Of course, you only create one cover letter and change the business name you are mailing it to.

Direct mailing is also a numbers game. If you figure up your costs, you will find each letter runs between 10 to 15 cents, including your business card cost, and a stamp is currently 42 cents. This type of ad is more expensive, but you are going after a business (commercial) account versus a private or residential account. In many cases, commercial accounts can provide more work for each visit which usually means more money.

You can also direct mail to specific subdivisions. There are companies that will sell you mailing information for specific subdivisions. A better way to obtain this type of mailing list is if you know a realtor or real estate broker personally. The real estate industry routinely generates lists like this. The reason for doing it by subdivision is that you can target specific income levels or residential lot sizes. If you want this type of information from a realtor, be prepared to refer some clients to them. Do your legwork first. Drive around and have 2 or 3 subdivision names that meet your criteria for your advertising campaign. Ask the realtor or broker politely for the lists, and then ask them for a few of their business cards. Make sure you hand them out, too. If they are willing to give you the information you ask for, be sure to say, "Thank you!"

Once you have the mailing list, prepare a letter that is as professional looking as you can possibly make it. Have a professional printer reproduce 1,000 copies. I recommend hand addressing the envelopes and placing individual stamps on them. Using a mailing label for your information would be a timesaver. Your greeting to the homeowner in the letter should be generic, but as warm as you can make it. Give information about what you do, how long you've been in business and generally speaking, how you determine pricing. I recommend seeing every job before giving a final bid. Again, advertising this way is more expensive, but you are targeting a specific demographic of people in a specific geographical area. Also, by mailing the ad versus driving out each day and walking 100 fliers, you save fuel.

I mentioned using a Chamber of Commerce membership list to find clients. You might also consider joining your local Chamber of Commerce. It's a great way to meet and network with local business owners in your town. There is usually some type of membership fee or dues required each year, but these can be written off on your taxes as a business expense. Also, there will be meetings you can attend that will keep you updated on changes that may affect your business in the local area.

Phone directories and the Yellow Pages have been around a long time. While I was on a window cleaning job one day a salesperson gave me her spiel while visiting my client to discuss upgrading HER Yellow Pages ad. During her presentation, it became clear there was a substantial discount being offered for the first year's ad. Again, if you have an advertising budget the Yellow Pages can be an effective way to spread the word about your business.

I learned about another type of advertising opportunity when I registered my knife sharpening business name with the State of Idaho. I started receiving ads in the mail from companies that sell refrigerator magnets, pens, calendars and other give-away items that come embossed with your company name, address, and contact information along with a logo if you have one. Of course, you spend money on these but they act like a business card. Insurance companies and realtors use them a lot. Promotional items are probably better utilized after your business is producing substantial income.

Newspapers, Thrifty Nickel or American Classified papers and other local publications are a good source of advertising.

Another interesting idea is renting a billboard along a main road. A female realtor in my area did just that. She rented a billboard on one of the busiest roads in my town. Having your picture, contact information and occupation plastered on a 20 by 60 foot sign definitely satisfies Bobby's admonition to "let everyone know who you are and what you do." Since this form of ad is expensive, you want to carefully consider the location before renting the sign. You want a lot of traffic going by. Commuters coming home from work sit in long lines during rush hour with little else to do but look at her picture and read her sign.

I was speaking with the owner of a local hair salon and spa while washing her windows. I had seen television ads for her business, so I asked her about the cost. While she wouldn't give dollar amounts, she commented that I would be surprised at how reasonable the prices were. She said her business had tripled since her TV ad started running. Again, you need to have an advertising budget to afford this, but it's just one possibility for getting the word out about your business. Thousands of people will see that ad every day!

When it comes to advertising for clients, you are only limited by your own initiative and creativity. Don't be shy! No one will work harder to build your business than you will.

Here's a mistake I made. *Never*, I repeat, *never* count on work someone says they might give you. If you don't have enough clients and someone has "promised" you work, keep advertising. Unless that person has committed to you in writing, don't sit around and count on it. Potential work that will tie up a significant amount of your time. Promises are just words. Like your business idea, it's not real until it's written down.

In seasonal businesses like lawn maintenance, there is a specific time frame for advertising and then you are working. If you fail to advertise during the window of opportunity because of a promise, and then the promised work doesn't materialize you will find it difficult to pick up jobs later.

I had a residential mowing client who was a builder. He and his partner suggested they could provide me $1,000 per week of lawn work in a new subdivision they were building. The deal they offered was I would mow their personal lawns for free in exchange for the work. I counted on that work and didn't spend time advertising. When I called the builder, his comment was, "Oh, that was just talk. At least for this summer the guys installing the sod will have the contract. We'll keep you in mind for next year though, depending on how these guys do. Sorry about that!" Sorry didn't help me build my business, but there was only one person at fault there—me. I'm sharing this hard learned lesson with you so you won't make the same mistake. Never count on a promise of work.

"Put in the time and you will make the money," another piece of wisdom from Bobby.

Chapter 7
Personal Appearance and Public Perception

I WOULD BE REMISS if I didn't bring up the concept of good personal appearance and grooming when trying to build up a small business. This is especially important if your target market is residential homeowners.

If you have numerous facial piercings, your arms and neck are covered with tattoos, you have multi-colored hair and your business idea is having a shop that offers those things, all is well. However, if you are planning on seeking work from homeowners (especially older ones) that look probably won't go over well.

Fair or not, first impressions really do matter. When marketing yourself to homeowners, having a neat clean-cut appearance will go a long way toward establishing credibility with them. Remember your goal: building a small business that will provide you with a living. Having a conservative hairstyle and dressing in a clean, neat way will help you accomplish that more quickly than insisting on being trendy or outrageous.

I typically wear fairly new jeans and a newer colored t-shirt or polo shirt when advertising. I try to have a new pair of cross training style shoes as well. Bobby likes to dress up more when he meets clients. Then again, he's a realtor and hair stylist. Both of those occupations are more formal and are primarily done indoors.

Another aspect of public perception is the appearance of your main work vehicle. There's absolutely nothing wrong with using an older automobile for your business. However, if your vehicle is dented up and the paint has seen better days, a little body work and a new paint job can be obtained at Maaco or other discount painters for as little as $300. The expense is a tax write-off, and can make a big difference in how clients perceive your business.

I had a small Nissan pickup a few years ago. I took it to Maaco and had some body work done and a metallic blue paint put on that still looked sharp six years later. Total cost, including body work, was under $400.

I have a final word about your vehicle. Once it's looking good with the dents out and a fresh coat of paint, I recommend washing it at least once a week if possible. A good looking rig presents a positive image to clients and potential clients. People notice these things. Maybe more importantly, people make decisions based on those observations.

If you grow your business to a point where you need to hire employees, I suggest you institute a dress code that your employees are required to meet while on the job. For example, no raggedy cut off jeans, no t-shirts with profanity or demonic images on them, no bare chests or flip-flop sandals. You want them to present a professional appearance for whatever type of work you do. Try to hire people who understand the importance of projecting a good public image for your company.

Chapter 8
Apprenticeship

WHETHER YOU ARE LEAVING something you've done for a long time to start a new career or find yourself out of work through a layoff, if there's a skill you've always thought would be a great thing to learn, this is a good time.

An *apprenticeship* is where you work with an experienced craftsman of a trade, for a period of time, with the intent of learning that trade from him. You can expect to earn an hourly wage (probably not the highest) and work hard. What you want to make sure of is that the craftsman you are working for is teaching you the trade, not just using you for cheap labor. You should be learning new things each week, not just doing the same job over and over—month after month.

Here locally I have a friend, Rick, in the sprinkler installation and repair business. Years back, he got a job working for someone in this trade and found that doing this work offered him some things he liked—being outside, working with his hands and, at times, some level of solitude. After spending 7 months with his first employer, he decided to go out and start his own business.

At this time he was married and his wife didn't understand (or support) his decision to go out on his own and give up the "security" of having steady employment working for someone else.

This is a great place to bring up an important issue that must be considered when deciding whether or not to become self-employed. If you are married or in a long-term committed relationship, your decision affects not only you but your partner. If you have always had a "job" working for someone else, making the transition to working for yourself can be a major change for your spouse or partner as well as for you. It is wise to spend time discussing the desire or need to start your own business with them, prior to making the decision. Outline what you want to do, why you want to do it and present research you've already done about your chosen business. Look at things like start-up costs, potential income, seasonal aspects if applicable, how long it will take, realistically, to earn what you are making now from your job. Seek your partner's buy-in to the decision before making it.

Rick actually called me back after giving me permission to use his experiences and recommended that I include the following part of his story. It deals with the issue above.

With 7 months of experience in sprinkler installation and repair, he decided to start his own business. Even though he was earning the same money from self- employment as he had been from his former boss, he found himself spending a lot of time learning on his jobs. Any mistakes he made during installation came out of his pocket. If he failed to account for things in the bidding process, he had to absorb those costs as well. Learning on the job was stressful. Coming home to a spouse who didn't support his original decision to become self-employed just added to the stress level. Sadly, the end result was that his marriage broke up.

He decided he needed more experience in the sprinkler business, so he went back to work as an employee and worked for two or three different employers for short stints. Then he landed a job with a boss he stayed with for seven years. During that time, he learned not only sprinkler installation and repair but control system installation, pump installation and repair and, of course, Spring system startups and Fall system blowouts. He learned everything he needed to know in order to be self-employed and was ready to start his own company—-again.

Over the seven year apprenticeship he served with his employer, he learned not only the technical side of his business, but by observing how his boss bid jobs and billed clients, he learned necessary business skills as well. He also observed which parts suppliers provided the best discounts and terms.

Another benefit of working in the same geographical area for seven years is that many people get to know you. When you go out on your own and start letting people know you have your own business, many will hire you for future projects because they know your quality of work from past jobs. He was able to hit the ground running with his second business.

My friend is an excellent example of two things—first, the concept of serving an apprenticeship. Second, he is a great example of something that everyone has experienced some people more than once. He failed at something, but rather than letting that determine his future, he went back to square one. He got financially stable again by doing whatever was necessary. Then he examined the failed venture to understand what factors caused him to fail. Once he understood those factors, Rick started planning to try again taking that information into account. The key here is <u>he tried again</u>.

I'm glad to report that Rick is now happily remarried and that his wife is also his business partner. She is obviously on board with owning their business. By taking the time to thoroughly learn the trade, learn from his past mistakes and by sharing his life with someone who is supportive of the idea of self-employment, his future is bright. Their current business is growing and he will soon be faced with the question of whether or not to hire employees.

If there is a trade you want to learn, look for someone doing that trade who needs a helper and is willing to teach you. Take careful notes as you learn. Don't just settle for learning the actual skills of doing the work but observe how your boss bids jobs, deals with customers, keeps his books and as many of the other factors that go into running a business as you can.

Being a craftsman is good. Learning how to be a business owner who is ALSO a craftsman is the key to building a successful business.

Chapter 9
Buying a Franchise

MY COUSIN GREG SPENT A number of years working in a privately owned family business (not his family). He had reason believe he might be made manager there at some point. When it became apparent that wasn't going to happen, he started looking at other options.

One of his friends heard he was thinking about starting his own business and suggested he look into buying a franchise. Conveniently, this friend happened to be a *franchise broker*. Franchise brokers work like any other broker—-they have a number of franchise options for sale and tailor the business opportunity to the potential franchisee's goals and work preferences.

In order to determine what those are, the broker administers some questionnaires that ask specific questions, like how much do you want to earn per year, inside versus outside work, are you willing to travel outside your home area, is being flexible with your time important—-and many other factors.

Once the questionnaires are evaluated, the broker presents the potential franchisee with business opportunities based on his (or her) responses. In my cousin's case, the first business he looked into was a building maintenance franchise. During that time there was a family emergency and he shelved the whole thing until the crisis was over.

When he went back to the broker, he decided to look at options other than building maintenance. The one that best fit his stated priorities was a lawn fertilization company based in Illinois. He contacted the company and after some initial conversation the company insisted on flying Greg and his wife back to corporate headquarters in Illinois. The company paid airfare, lodging and car rental. The purpose of the visit was what they called "discovery day." This day was designed to give Greg, his wife and the owners an opportunity to meet each other. It wouldn't surprise me if this company turned down some applicants based on their impressions of the candidate during this discovery process.

My cousin was given a list of current franchise holders and encouraged to call any or all of them with questions—-anything he wanted to know about the company, how the individual franchise holders did business, their advertising strategies, how they felt about the company—literally anything. He did this and liked what he heard.

The participation in "discovery day" and the whole experience of going back to the corporate headquarters is called *due diligence*. Anyone considering investing in anything should go through this process. If you decide to look into buying a franchise and the company seems more interested in your money than in you, as a person who will be representing their business, think twice about buying in. The fact that my cousin and his wife were flown to Illinois and "wined and dined" at the company's expense—and that the owners were willing to have him speak with other people who already held franchises said good things about how they do business. Encouraging his wife to come was also a good business decision. It gave the company an opportunity to gauge her support of Greg's move into self-employment. As stated in the previous chapter, having your life partner's "buy-in" before making a decision to start your own business can be a key factor in success or failure.

After looking at the business opportunity and meeting the company's owners, Greg decided to buy the franchise. He purchased a pickup truck and the company outfitted it with the basic equipment he would need to get started. There were equipment upgrades available, but Greg decided to start with the basics. Once the truck was ready, he flew back to Illinois and drove the truck to Idaho.

Part of the franchise he purchased was a first year blanket advertising campaign. The cost of the advertising was included in the initial purchase price and was non-negotiable. One of the most important things to a new franchise is getting off to a quick start. A professionally run mail advertising campaign in the new service area is a great idea.

In addition, the company supplied all the business cards, door hangers, bid sheets, yard signs and plastic stakes, billing materials and pre-sized plastic bags that he needed to get started. He also received intense training on the basics of the fertilization business—-use of chemicals and application methods, safety precautions and best practices for efficiency.

Through continuing education, he has added tree spraying and pest control to his list of services provided. He also added aeration (the machine that punches those holes and leaves plugs in lawns). Other courses are available through local colleges and he takes advantage of them, especially during the winter.

Next, his company supplied him with a business plan that showed him year by year benchmarks based on what other franchise holders had accomplished across the country. He was able to see after his first year, where he was in relation to where the company projected him to be. At the end of his first season, he went back to the Illinois headquarters to analyze his first year and received coaching and suggestions for faster growth, more effective marketing strategies and the possibility of upgrading to more automated equipment for more effective use of his time through increased efficiency.

Finally, the company supplied him with computer software set up specifically for his franchise. He can chart his client base, work performed, payments received, outstanding bills, expense and probably profit and loss on a daily basis. There's also a great map generating package that he can use to print out his daily route for work if he's unfamiliar with a new client's location. All in all, what the system can do is pretty amazing!

I sat down with him and asked him what he thought about his decision after three years of running the business. He said, "I'm thirty-seven now. I wish I'd started this at twenty-five. The way things are going, there's a good chance that by now I'd have 6 or 7 trucks and between 5 and 10 full time employees. Each truck would probably generate at least $100,000 per year in gross earnings."

Buying a franchise jump starts your business. However, before you spend any money, make sure you ask the hard questions:

1. What is supplied by the company?
2. What support is available?
3. What is the initial cost?
4. Are there yearly costs beyond that?
5. How much do you have to pay for the necessary paperwork items (business cards, estimate sheets, billing invoices, fliers, etc.)?
6. What is the cost of equipment you will need to get started?

This is one of those times where there are NO stupid questions. Make sure you have everything in writing. If you are looking into a franchise opportunity and at any point hear something or see something that makes you uneasy or suspicious, be careful. If you ask questions and don't get direct, professional answers, be VERY careful. This is a big investment and you want to buy into a company that has a good track record and a lot of happy franchisees. In fact, I would suggest asking for that list of current franchise holders, like my cousin was given by his company, so you can speak to them before making a decision. I would think a well established franchise owner would be happy to have you speak with his other franchisees before making a large financial investment in his business.

Buying a franchise requires a large initial investment. This is called *overhead*. For a franchise to be successful, you must be able to earn enough to pay living expenses AND pay down your overhead costs. Too much debt can kill any business—-small or large.

There are advantages and disadvantages to every type of business. With franchises, the biggest disadvantage is the buy-in cost. On the upside, the business is laid out for you. It comes with a step-by-step action plan.

If you received a large buy out from your previous employer or recently came into a sizeable inheritance, buying a franchise might be a way for you to go.

Chapter 10
Sales

THERE ARE MANY DIFFERENT ways to be self-employed in sales—owning a store or shop, drive-through espresso stand, bodega or even door to door sales. That said, I want to start smaller and share what I've learned later in life. If I sell an item to someone who wants it, I just made the easiest money I can make. Minimal physical labor and in most cases they will come to where I am, and if I receive more than I paid I even made a profit. By the way, not all sales need to be profitable in order to be good. I am going to break this chapter into sections.

SMALL SALES

I'm willing to bet that you have many small items at home that you either don't need, don't use or don't want and each one of them is taking up space that could be used for other purposes. I'm even willing to bet there are some of you who have storage units you're renting that are packed with exactly the type of items I'm talking about.

Here's my challenge to you: go through your home and evaluate everything you own. Are you actually using things? How many items are tucked away on shelves, in closets or stored under the counter in your kitchen that haven't seen the light of day in over a year? How about your garage or shop? Do you have enough Christmas decorations for your entire block? Are you in your 50's or 60's and have camping gear you haven't even thought about in thirty years?

Look: if you have enough money to purchase five to ten acres in or near a town and can afford to construct a storage facility, that facility can BE your self-employment venture.

On the other hand, if you are renting space to store items you aren't using, I'll issue the same challenge. Go to your storage unit and take inventory of what's there. Be as objective as you can and try to give each item a fair market value (what you could reasonably expect to sell it as used). In many cases you've probably already paid more in storage fees than the total value of what is being stored.

If you accept my challenge and go through everything you own, I guarantee you will have piles of things you aren't using or don't need. It's time to participate in an American tradition—-yard sales.

Earlier I made the statement that not all sales need to be profitable in order to be good. Yard and garage sales is what I meant. You probably won't even come close to getting what you paid for those items, but if they are things you don't use anymore, who cares? Every one of them you sell creates income. The object of being self-employed is to earn income by yourself, for yourself.

I urge you to sell or donate everything you have in your storage unit. This will create two income streams—the money you earn through sales or a tax write off for donations plus you are saving what you've been paying for rent space. Ben Franklin was a smart guy, he said, "A penny saved is a penny earned." It's true. Why pay a monthly fee to store unused things?

I recently sold a gun safe. There was a time earlier in life when I owned as many as six firearms. I felt it was necessary to lock them up in case of a burglary. Since I sold off the firearms, the safe became unnecessary. I originally paid $899 new and another $100 to have the safe delivered and installed in my basement. I sold it for $650 cash eleven years later. Did I make a profit? No. Was it a good sale? Absolutely! I didn't need it any more and it was blocking about a third of my garage as I had it sitting right inside the garage door so I could easily show it to potential buyers.

This is a personal example of selling off possessions that aren't used or needed. I must say, it was the easiest $650 I ever made. My advertising method was a sign on the corner that said GUN SAFE and my address. It took about six months to sell, but

I only put the sign out on the corner on days I was going to be at home anyway. Many of those days I was working on this book. The buyer came where I was to look at the safe. Once we agreed on a price he showed up with cash, a truckload of helpers and a trailer. He paid me and they loaded it up. I counted the money. You must admit, that was pretty easy for me.

If you accept my challenge and de-clutter your home and your life, I am certain you will start seeing the value of selling things to make money as a side business.

There are many people who invest a few hours on weekends driving around their towns looking for yard and garage sales or going to local auctions. They are looking for items other people are trying to get rid of which they can purchase inexpensively and resell at a profit. I've started doing this. It's a simple way to incorporate sales into your life whether you are an employee for someone else or self-employed.

Instead of thinking about money in terms of the salary from your job, or income from your business, think of money in terms of income streams. The more income streams you can establish the better chance you have of becoming financially independent. Holding a yard sale every couple of months is relatively simple, your customers come to you and each sale creates an income stream. Over the course of a year, this can easily result in $1,000 to $2,000 in additional income.

Don't be shy about seeking out items for resale. If you have family or friends who say they want to get rid of old items, volunteer to haul them away.

Be up front about the fact that you are going to try to resell them. In many cases, people don't care—-they just want the things gone. Make a point of telling people you are willing to haul away unwanted usable things at any time. Every usable item you can acquire free is potential income.

My advice about selling pretty much anything (especially to strangers) is to only accept cash. If the potential buyer absolutely insists on paying with a check, offer to drive them to their bank, if the item being sold is a big ticket item. If it's a smaller item, offer to set the item back for an hour so they can visit an ATM. If you accept a check and it bounces your goods are gone and collecting on bad checks from strangers can be a real pain. The simplest way to avoid the problem is just refuse to accept a check in payment.

LARGER SALES

In discussing larger sales, I'm targeting things like my gun safe example—sales in the hundreds or thousands of dollars. In fact, I think I'll include properties in this section as well.

As you go through life, there are opportunities all around you. For instance, have you ever had a co-worker mention they had a car for sale? Did you look into what kind of car it was? Did you ask any questions about either the vehicle or why they wanted to sell it? If not, why not?

Every time someone is selling something, it is a potential income stream for you. What you need to do is start looking at things that way. For example, why are they selling the car? By asking a couple of questions, you may find that the family has a pressing financial need and selling the vehicle quickly will resolve their need. Say you look into it and the car they are selling is listed in the Kelly Blue Book (low book value) at $4,000. You look at the car, it starts right up and had obviously been well taken care of. No major dents, the interior is in good shape and it runs well. They are asking $1,000 cash. This is an opportunity!

If you are financially able, buy the car. You resolve their immediate need and give yourself the opportunity to create an income stream. If the low book value is $4,000, print out that information and tape it on the car window next to your "For Sale" sign. Ask for the low book price and be willing to take maybe $2,500. Even if it takes ten months to sell the vehicle, you will earn over $100 per month if offered your bottom dollar amount. I'm deducting a little from your eventual sale price because it would make sense to detail the car before placing it out for sale. Wash and wax it, completely clean the interior, use a dashboard polish on the dash and other plastic panels and use a tire treatment on the tires to shine them up. Might cost $100 total. Probably less if you do it all yourself.

The above example can be duplicated for any item or group of items where you can go out and do research on market values.

At the next level are properties. One of the fastest ways to make a large amount of money quickly is to be the first person to learn that a property owner is in financial difficulty and is facing the possibility of foreclosure. This is not an opportunity to take advantage of someone else's misery. If you are compassionate and handle it right, it is an opportunity to let them walk away with their credit intact and cash in their pocket to help them start over again.

This is a win, win, win. Why three wins? The seller's credit is somewhat salvaged, you gain a property with a fair amount of equity already present and the bank doesn't have to deal with a foreclosure. Believe it or not, banks don't want houses back. They're not in the business of selling houses. They are in the loan business. Foreclosure generates a lot of extra work for lending institutions. They would much rather have the cash.

Here's an opportunity for those who don't mind moving every two to three years and are relatively handy. A few years back the government changed tax laws to allow people to sell properties they have lived in as their primary residence for 2 or more years without paying capital gains taxes. For those willing to look for a "fixer-upper" they can live in while they rehabilitate the property for resale, it can be very profitable. As an example, say someone finds a property in an area where the average value is $200,000. They are able to buy the most rundown house in the area for $150,000.

Assuming most of the repairs are cosmetic and they have the skills to do a lot of the work themselves, this is a great opportunity. In fact, I could see some younger couples moving every two or three years and making a substantial income stream from these activities. Bear in mind, if they purchased the property at $150,000 and spent two years bringing it up to the same quality as the surrounding homes, it's not unreasonable to expect an appraisal equal to the surrounding properties. Also, in two years property values most likely will have gone up some. If they realized a $60,000 increase (or more) at the sale of the property, they just earned $30,000 per year with no tax penalty.

Real estate is one of the best ways to make large sums of money over time. Of course, contrary to many infomercials it is difficult to make this type of deal without at least some cash. I'm not saying it's impossible to get a property "no money down," I'm saying that by spending time and looking for undervalued properties that need work and having either cash or a credit line available, many more opportunities will present themselves.

Here's another type of sales opportunity. Do you use and believe in Avon products? Why not sell them on the side? How about Beauty Control cosmetic products? Why not become a representative as a sideline? Any product you use regularly and believe in based on personal experience is a great product to sell. The best sales tool known to man is personal testimony. If you believe in a product, your potential customer will pick that up as you speak with them.

The internet has made selling things easier. PayPal allows people from everywhere to pay for online purchases by facilitating the transaction regardless of the seller's country or currency used. With the advent of ebay and other online auction sites, and Craigslist or other free online classified sites there's no reason a person can't sell things nationwide. In fact, with not too much more effort a person can sell things world wide—literally.

Let me introduce you to my friend Gary. He had a job working for a food distribution corporation and after a year was very disillusioned. The starting pay wasn't great and after a year his first pay increase was $.25 per hour. That equates to $10 per week. Horrid! He toiled away for another year, but after another raise of $.75 per hour, he decided he needed to do something different. He had tried selling things on ebay earlier in life, but hadn't been met with much success. One day, he had an epiphany (an AHA! moment), he realized that in earlier attempts at selling on ebay his biggest problem was poor record keeping. He never knew if he'd made a profit or not. Fortunately, he was good at creating spreadsheets and creating the formulas that make them work.

He sat down and created an Excel spreadsheet that took into account many variables. He started selling "out of print" Dungeons and Dragons items online. At first things went slowly.

However, due to his spreadsheet, in 6 months he was able to see that he was making a profit. He was making enough money that he decided to give notice at his job and work his ebay business full time.

To date, I believe his best month (net profit) was a little over $1,000 on around $3,000 in gross sales. That's hard to believe considering that what he's doing is bidding on auctions on ebay, getting the ones he wins home, grading them, repackaging them (this actually has a name—*amalgamating*) and reselling them for profit. Best of all, the only time he needs to leave home is to go to the post office to mail out customer orders or to go pick up packaging materials. Surprisingly, a fair percentage of his customers live outside the U.S.A. He says at least 33% of his sales are to overseas customers. That's amazing! The amount of paperwork required to ship overseas is minimal and just like here, the customer pays for shipping.

If Gary can do this, there are many other people who can do it. In fact there are many people doing it right now and making their entire living at it. If you can buy it, you can find it on ebay. If people are selling it there and you know the value of things, you can win auctions at prices that allow you to resell at a profit. My buddy is living proof of this.

There are many wholesalers out there who will sell you items at a substantial discount. SMC has over 3,000 items available. They will even drop-ship the items to your customers in your business name. I'm not endorsing SMC, but I've watched their infomercial enough times to realize that if you are willing to do the leg work, they are a decent product supplier. If you type the words "wholesale suppliers" into any search engine, you will probably have to spend a week reading through all the wholesalers that pop up.

SALES CAREERS

For someone who wants to be self-employed and doesn't want to do physical labor, commission sales are a good choice. It helps to be comfortable talking to people. Self-employment in sales includes anyone who works in an industry where they are paid strictly on commission.

Some of the perks in this area include working indoors, dressing well, temperature-controlled environment, possibility of bonuses based on meeting or exceeding sales goals, spending time around things you like (a sports car lover who sells them for instance) and finally not doing physical labor or exchanging hours for dollars.

In sales, any given day has the potential to result in completed transactions that earn the salesperson large amounts of income (a realtor closing on a property transaction comes to mind). Of course, the downside is that if nothing is sold there is no income. It's not for everyone, but some of the most highly paid people in the world are top sales people. It's a career choice worth considering.

In writing this chapter, my goal has been to show that whether you run your own business or are employed by someone else, creating additional income streams through selling your own excess possessions or seeking out items to sell at a profit (up to and including properties) is a mindset. There are also many commission sales opportunities available to people who have the 'gift of gab.' If you have a way of making people feel like they've known you all their lives after 2 minutes, sales might be for you.

Many people go through life accumulating things. I guess they subscribe to the old joke "He who dies with the most toys, wins." When they are gone, their relatives are left to dispose of it all. Much is given away, sold for next to nothing, donated to charity or just thrown in the trash. I've personally witnessed this in my own family, so I know it's true. Save your family the work. Sell the excess now for profit or donate it for a tax write-off to a charity. De-clutter your home and your life. It's a good thing.

Chapter 11
Time Management

NOW THAT YOU'VE GONE out and developed a clientele and are working, being an effective time manager is crucial. It can make or break your small business. With time, unlike many other things in life, once a second, minute or hour is gone it can't be replaced. Every minute is valuable and every minute counts.

Before you start making a list of every single work related thing you can think of and molding your world around that, stop! Mom has a favorite expression, "I work to live, I don't live to work." The older I get the more I see the wisdom of that.

To begin the process of managing your time, look at your life. What things are important to you—family, friends, church, exercise, entertainment, pets, continuing education? Before charting your work schedule, you need to figure out what your REAL priorities are. Set aside time for family, friends, church and the other things in your life which aren't work related. Then figure out how to make your work schedule fit in with those priorities.

I have to confess, Bobby wrote this chapter. Well, he gave me the outline. I wouldn't even have considered planning the other parts of my life first. I'm single. I have no family living with me, no kids and currently no pets. Bobby has all those things in his busy life and manages to make it all work. It works because he consciously plans time for each area of his life.

Once you have your non-work life written down and can look at each area, then start with a work day. Making and using a list each day can save you a lot of time, especially if you have many appointments. After you finish a job or appointment, check it off the list. Seeing that checkmark is an added assurance that you didn't miss an appointment. Missed appointments are almost always bad. In most businesses, they can cost you money and clients.

Depending on what it is you do, try to allow large enough blocks of time for each job to accommodate things like driving time, changing clothes, or possibly speaking with the client for a few minutes (have to be careful with this one). There's a delicate balance between being efficient with your time and having good business owner to client relationships. A couple of minutes spent chatting with the person who is paying your bills is good public relations. After giving a client a few minutes of your time, don't be afraid to say, "It's been nice talking with you, but I have to get going." Most people will understand that you have more jobs to do.

One of the biggest potential distractions during a working day can be personal phone calls. Try to convey to family and friends that when you are out working they should call only in an emergency. Picking up a gallon of milk on the way home does not constitute an emergency. If your home phone has voicemail, encourage them to call that number and leave a message with the understanding that you will call them when you are done with your work day. Of course, then you need to make sure to check those messages every day and actually return those calls. Another good way for family and friends to communicate with you is through e-mails. Again, this means you need to be diligent in checking and responding to them.

Being forced to stop working to deal with personal issues during a work day can cost more than the actual minutes the calls take. The effect is exponential. Here's why—-when you are working, especially if the work you do is repetitive, you get into a rhythm, a flow. Every time that flow is interrupted by something like a personal call, you lose the momentum and have to start over. At the beginning of the day when you are fresh, if the flow is uninterrupted you can really get things done effectively. If you are interrupted early in the day, it is easier to get back up to speed. As the day wears on and you start getting tired, each interruption costs more time because it is increasingly more difficult to get back up to speed.

If you work for yourself and by yourself, develop a habit of taking lunch breaks and coffee breaks if you want them, at more or less the same times each day. It's kind of funny——you want to be efficient and manage your time while also remaining flexible to accommodate unexpected things. As you continue in your self-employment effort you will understand the principles being proposed in this chapter better. It's important to be efficient. It is also important to be flexible. The key here is for YOU to decide how and when to be flexible, NOT your clients or family or friends.

Each person is different, but as I pointed out earlier regardless of what type of person you are, there are only so many minutes in a day. Once one of them is used (productively or non-productively) it is gone. Having a work schedule that is built around the core non-work parts of your life can at least help you manage the interruptions and maintain a workable level of efficiency.

When you worked for a boss, he took care of most of these things by dictating your work area, your breaks, whether or not using the phone for personal calls was allowed, when to be at work, when to go home, etc. Now it's all on you. It's a good thing—and by practicing good time management skills, you can be efficient AND flexible. Both of these things will help you to be successful.

Chapter 12
Taxes

THIS CHAPTER WILL BE short, but important. Pay attention if you want to avoid stress.

As you venture into self-employment, especially if you are coming out of a lifetime of working as an employee, one of the easiest mistakes to make is not preparing to set aside and pay your own self-employment taxes. The second most common mistake is not setting aside enough. It's an easy error to make, since you've always had your income taxes deducted for you by an employer. All you had to do was decide how many dependents to claim. Now you are your employer.

I made this mistake. My current accountant assured me I wasn't the first and wouldn't be the last person who failed to properly plan their self-employment tax strategy. I'm hoping this chapter will help you avoid learning more about the IRS (the hard way) than you need to. Trust me here—it's not fun.

My first recommendation is to hire an accountant. Sit down with them and ask them to educate you about how much you need to set aside, what kind of records you need to keep and how to keep them so you are efficiently organized when tax time rolls around. Most accountants use a set of forms that summarize each area of deductions your particular business might use. Ask for a set from the previous year so you can familiarize yourself with them for the coming tax year. Even if your accountant charges you a consultation fee for this sit-down meeting, pay it. It's a tax write-off and unless you are willing to spend many hours every year reading the latest IRS tax policy for the self-employed, a good accountant's advice is worth every penny they charge.

One of the best write-offs you can have if you own your own residence is a home office. This may also apply if you are a renter. Ask your accountant. I've been self-employed for six years and this will be the first year I have a room dedicated as a home office. Not doing this sooner was a big mistake on my part that cost me hundreds of dollars in self-employment taxes paid unnecessarily.

A simple illustration follows. You have a 1200 square foot house. One bedroom (your office) measures 10' X 12' (120 square feet.) That's 10 percent of the total square footage of the house. What that means is that you can deduct 10 percent of your mortgage, insurance, water/sewer/trash bill, gas bill, wood cost if you heat with wood, improvements to the whole house like a new roof, more efficient windows for the house, new siding, painting etc. That's basically 10 percent of everything. It's a big deal! I estimate I'll be able to write off $1,000 this tax year.

Take advantage of every single tax break available! Every dollar you don't pay in taxes is a dollar in your pocket. Remember Ben Franklin—"a penny saved is a penny earned." Would you rather save or spend that money yourself, or let the IRS collect it and the U.S. Government spend it? Easy call for me!

Here's my spiel about honesty. With all the tax write-offs available to the self- employed, there's no reason to cheat on your taxes. If you work hard and stay busy, you should be able to earn enough from your self-employment efforts to take care of your needs and pay your fair share of taxes. I'm not the morality police, but I can tell you I feel truly blessed to be able to earn a living as a self-employed person and know that I'm doing so honestly.

My businesses are lawn maintenance, window cleaning and knife and garden implement sharpening. I am not an accountant. What makes sense to me is hiring someone whose job includes keeping up with all the changes year to year in the tax code. That doesn't mean I don't review their work once my taxes have been prepared.

Each year I sit down with them and ask questions. Hire someone to prepare the tax return for you, but don't abdicate your own responsibility to understand what they are doing. Knowledge is power. When it comes to dealing with the IRS, I've learned the hard way that it's my responsibility as a self-employed person to have as much knowledge as possible—even if I do use an accountant.

Being CEO of your own small business means that you are in charge of doing everything yourself, or subcontracting parts of your business to experts in that area. Tax advice and preparation is a good one to subcontract out. Don't forget all the fees associated with doing this are a tax write-off.

Chapter 13
Clients

WHEN YOU START YOUR own business, you are the boss. If you come from a background where you were always an employee, this concept may seem like heaven. In practice, however, making the transition from employee to self-employed business owner can be challenging.

As you start dealing with clients who hire you to provide them with your service or trade, you must always remember that they are clients—not your bosses. There are some fundamental differences between being an employee and being a business owner. Let's discuss some of them.

First, when you hire on with a company as an employee, they tell you what tasks you will perform. Next, they dictate what you will be paid as a starting wage. You are told what shift you will work and how many hours you will work per shift. You are told when to take breaks and for how long. Basically, every aspect of your work is dictated to you. Your responsibility is to show up on time and do whatever you are told on your scheduled days and throughout your work period.

As a self-employed person, you decide what work you will or will not perform. You schedule what days you will or won't work. You schedule each client's job. You decide how much you will charge for your service or trade. Taking lunch or rest breaks is your decision. In almost total opposition to being an employee, you decide every aspect of your work day.

Where it gets complicated is when you aren't secure in being your own boss. The first thing you must master in dealing with clients is self-assurance. Without being confrontational you need to be able to project a professional and confident persona to those you work for or hope to work for.

I can assure you, from my own personal experience, that you will run into many different situations while dealing with clients that will challenge your willingness to be the boss. There are many people out there who think that if they are paying you money, THEY are your boss. Not so. In fact, this is one of the main things you need to discourage as a business owner when dealing with clients or potential clients. I advocate calm, respectful but firm insistence when deciding on certain things, like what you will charge for your service, when (what day) the work will be performed, exactly what work will be performed and method and time of payment.

Here are some things I've run into during my years as a self-employed person, then I'll go back and address each one specifically:

1. Haggling over your bid price and attempting to drive it down.
2. Demanding a specific day for service.
3. Demanding a specific time for service.
4. Expecting you to add services with no additional compensation.
5. Asking that you work up a written bid and leave it without meeting them.
6. Clients making changes to your agreement unilaterally without your input.
7. NOT PAYING IN A TIMELY MANNER!!

HAGGLERS

When you give an estimate, if possible insist on looking at the work when the homeowner is at the residence. If that's just not possible, get a callback number, drive out and look at the work and while you are still at the job site, call the homeowner with your bid and verbally list the exact tasks you will perform for that amount of money. If the homeowner is there when you give your bid, it is helpful to have a pre-printed handout that outlines the tasks included in your basic service. If the client wants things done that you don't do, tell them so up front. I've almost always regretted taking on work I really didn't want to do. If they want to add things you are willing to do, but are unwilling to pay more for those services, respectfully say no.

During your first year of self-employment, you should be able to determine the costs of providing your service. Once you have a good idea of those costs, you need to adjust your pricing structure to reflect those costs and build in a good profit. You are in business to make a good living, not to save your clients money. If price is their motivator, let them get someone else. I live by the following rule—-I will not be the low cost provider of any service or trade. Why? The low cost providers will always work their tails off and make less money than people who demand a fair rate for their work. I can charge a third more money, work a third less jobs and make the same money as a "low cost provider," while providing the same or better service.

SPECIFIC DAY

In many businesses (especially service businesses) there are certain days that are in high demand. Thursday and Friday are popular as they fall right before the weekend. Most people work during the week and like their houses clean, lawns mowed, etc. so they can enjoy them while they are off on the weekend. Still, as you build up a clientele you will get to a point where each day is filled up. At that point, when you get called for a bid, during the conversation let callers know which days you have available. If they just want the work done, they won't care. If a specific day really matters to them, they'll call someone else.

Maybe I'm old fashioned, but I try not to be a "respecter of persons." For instance, if I'm fully booked on a given day (say Friday) and a prospective client with a potentially lucrative job is insisting on that day, I won't automatically accept the new job at the expense of my existing clients. Those folks have helped me pay my bills for years. If I can work out an accommodation where an existing client is willing to move to a different day, great! If not, I thank the potential client for contacting me, but tell them Friday is not available.

SPECIFIC TIME

In my lawn business, I never guarantee a specific time that I will provide service. Equipment breaks down, emergencies happen, an opportunistic job presents itself (someone going out of town that day and wanting a one time mow, for example). I schedule that business so that my clients know which day I'll be there. I do like consistency, so as much as possible I try to maintain the same schedule. I just refuse to guarantee it.

On the other hand, in a business like window cleaning where it's a one time job (not weekly), I will give a specific day and time and if something comes up so I can't make it or will be late, I call immediately and let the client know.

ADDITIONAL SERVICES FOR FREE

When either a prospective or existing client tries to pressure you into adding tasks to your service without any additional compensation, use some common sense. If someone you have a good working relationship with asks you to do a small favor that will take 5 minutes or less, common sense says "Sure, glad to help out." Say it with a smile. You know there's a problem if these requests become a regular thing. Stick to your original agreement with clients. If they want to change the agreement by adding work you are willing to do, renegotiate your fee. Never allow yourself to get pushed into work you don't want to do.

When I was younger I would pull weeds. I'm talking about getting on my knees with a short handled shovel and digging those things out of there. I no longer do that because it makes my back hurt. When asked, I simply tell folks I don't do that. The same holds true for any work I don't want to do. After all I own the business.

WRITTEN ESTIMATES

I learned the hard way in my window cleaning business that when clients ask you to drive by their home while they are at work, complete a written estimate and leave it on the door—it's a serious mistake. Here's why. There are unethical (in my opinion) large companies who will offer to beat any written estimate by a small percentage. Homeowners who know this get self-employed people like me to drive out (wasting my time, fuel and effort) and leave a written estimate while they are at work. They then call the large company and get the job done by them for a "discounted" price. Two things about this bother me. First, the homeowner probably never seriously intended to use my service. Second, the large company just sits by the phone and "steals" jobs I went out and hustled for. I know it's not really stealing, but these companies essentially do nothing to earn the job. I think it's unethical.

The way to avoid all this is when working up an estimate, do everything possible to meet the homeowner at their residence. If this just isn't possible, get a callback number and from the job site call the owner and give a verbal bid for the work. If they are truly interested in having you do the job that should be sufficient. Be suspicious if they are doggedly insistent that you leave a written estimate. Offer them a written invoice at the agreed on price once you've completed the work. If they use that to get their "discount" on future jobs, well at least you got paid the first time.

UNNEGOTIATED CHANGES

During your initial meeting with a potential client on repeat jobs (housecleaning, lawn maintenance, child care—-to name a few), don't forget to make clear your season parameters or the minimum number of times per week or month that you will provide your service for the price.

In my lawn mowing business, I mow only on a weekly basis. No every other week or "skip a week" jobs. Starting with the 2008 mowing season I asked clients to agree in advance that the season would run mid-April through the end of September on a weekly basis. After that, if the client wants every other week service or to stop service altogether, that's fine. In your business, negotiate terms you can live with. If a client agrees to a specific arrangement and then at a later date decides to change the terms, be willing to walk away from the work if they won't renegotiate the fee.

TIMELY COMPENSATION

Being compensated in a timely manner is the number one thing every self-employed person should insist on. Also, this is something you should dictate. I have had more frustration over this one issue in self-employment than any other (with the possible exception of tax trouble). Here's what I suggest. In a business where you are working weekly, try to have the client agree to pay weekly. If they strongly prefer being billed monthly offer to invoice in the second week of the month, with payment to be received no later than the last day of the month. Anyone living in or near your town will be able to post a check to you within 14 days. If you have clients who agree to this arrangement and then are late, I suggest a polite but firm reminder for the following month. If they are late again, I suggest telling them you need to be paid for the month in advance or on a weekly basis from that point forward. It may cost a client, but will save frustration.

Unfortunately, I had some people pay me late consistently (sometimes as much as a month late) for years. In 2007 I got fed up. Until then I had been invoicing at the end of the month. About 90 percent of my clients paid in a timely manner. The other 10 percent were habitually late. Being forced into making collection calls was not why I got into self-employment. I changed my invoicing policy from the end of the month to the second week each month and personally explained to each and every client why. That one change almost eliminated the late payment issue.

Instead of being angry about things like this in your business, don't wait five years like I did to make a proactive change. Here's another idea I got from a client, which will eliminate all the collection hassles. Offer a small discount (5 or 10 percent) to any client who will prepay for the season. If you have takers, don't forget to grab a calendar and put down on the invoice you write them for their check exactly what weeks are covered. An example would be, "This invoice covers mowing service from April 15 through September 30. Any service provided after September 30 will be on a week to week basis at $35.00 per visit." Having clients prepay is great. Of course, then you are obligated to show up every week and provide service. It's well worth being obligated. No collection hassles.

If you've read carefully, you will note that over the years I've learned to be much more direct with clients. I'll admit that part of that comes from building up a clientele large enough that I can afford to drop a client here or there. When you are first starting out, you may have to put up with some of these behaviors for awhile. As your business grows, keep track of those clients who are difficult. Once you can afford to, start letting them go. Seriously! Life is too short to work for people who make things difficult.

In six years, I can count the clients who fall into this category on one hand. Of all the people I've worked with, that is a small number. Most people are considerate and realize you have to make a living. If you do your job well and show up consistently, the vast majority of your clients will be loyal— even when you raise your rates in reasonable increments.

My advice is that if you are contacted by people who are looking for the low cost provider, let 'em get someone else. If an existing client threatens you with the loss of work if you won't add additional tasks for the same price, let them go. Most importantly, if you have someone who consistently can't seem to find their checkbook to pay you in a timely manner, or bounces a check more than once, dump them RIGHT NOW! There is no excuse for people who receive your service or trade work to stall about paying you. It's rude—especially if it's habitual. You will be better off not working for them.

To summarize, most clients will be very happy to keep you working for them if your show up consistently and provide a decent quality of work. It's your responsibility to make clear from the start of the work relationship exactly what your service consists of and how much it costs, when the work will be performed and when they are expected to pay you. Once you reach agreement, it's your responsibility to provide the service regularly and their responsibility to pay you regularly and in a timely manner.

In the end, it really is your business. By having many clients instead of one boss, you have the latitude to part ways with uncooperative clients and still make a good living. Being your own boss is a good thing once you gain the confidence in your ability. Be respectful to clients, but always remember who's in charge—you!

Chapter 14
Dealing with Frustration

LET'S FACE IT——-AT times, in life, we all get frustrated. There are those rare people who always seem to be cheerful regardless of their circumstances. They never seem to be upset about anything. They never seem to be frustrated. Some are truly at peace with life. Others are just good actors.

For most of us, frustration is a normal part of every day life. In self-employment how you deal with it can make a huge difference, not only in how fast your business grows, but ultimately in whether your business is a success or failure.

Rather than quote from many well known books that promote a positive attitude, I'm going to share a real life experience from my lawn maintenance business last season. Not dealing with frustration in a productive manner cost me $1,200 annually. Read and learn.

I have magnetic advertising for my lawn business on my truck. I got a call on my cell phone from a man sitting next to me in traffic. It was late in the season and he was looking for someone to finish out the mowing season for him and to take over on a full time basis in the spring. I got the address and driving directions from him. The next day, I drove out and took a look at his yard. He had a slightly larger than average lot. There was a lot of edging work——-more than normal.

During the previous week, I'd had three clients call, who wanted to cut back service in August due to the heat. I was frustrated about that as it meant lost income. There were also some other issues I was dealing with at that time. Bottom line——- when I called the potential client from his property and started speaking with him, my mind was on a number of issues that had absolutely nothing to do with the guy on the phone.

He asked me how much I would charge. It was a simple question. I justified a price of $45 per week. During the conversation leading up to that, I made the negotiation process much longer and more involved than necessary. Looking back, it's easy to see I was frustrated with other people and other things.

I remember his exact words. "I'm sensing a lot of complications here. I just want my lawn mowed. I have no problem paying $45 per week, but…I'm going to go with my gut here…I think I'll pass."

This total stranger, not knowing me from Adam—-in fact, never having met me face to face could sense through the phone line that something was off about me. There was something that just wasn't right so he went with his gut.

I thanked him for his interest in my business and concluded the call. I was left standing on the sidewalk staring at my phone. I asked myself a question. "What just happened?" As I stood there, it was like I heard a little gong in my head and I could see a movie screen in my mind. On the screen was an entire day spent rehashing different frustrations. The end result of my bad coping skills and a lifetime habit of replaying negative situations over and over was the loss of a job worth $1200 per year.

Now all this happened in about thirty seconds standing there in 95 degree heat in that subdivision. Sometimes in life good <u>can</u> come out of bad. I realized that day that probably a lot of areas in my life were negatively affected by my bad habit of replaying frustrations day after day.

I've finally started a process of eliminating that bad habit. Notice, I said I've "started." It usually takes time and effort to change a life long pattern of negative behavior. The first step in changing is to admit the habit exists. By acknowledging it out loud you stop practicing denial. Denial is a powerful mindset that is at the root of many destructive life habits. By verbally admitting those negative and potentially destructive habits to yourself, and possibly to selected other people in your life, you free yourself to start changing them.

Why share this personal failure with you? In part, to show you that in self-employment you must find a constructive way to deal with frustration. Not doing so can cost you clients and income. If negative personal traits or life's typical frustrations aren't dealt with in an effective manner, they can cost you the ability to earn a living as a business owner.

Another aspect is the positive potential this experience shows. No matter what the negative things in your life are, you can always choose to change them. If you watch movies at all, you've probably heard the following proverb, "A journey of a thousand miles starts with a single step." In real life, it's true.

When a frustrating situation develops, deal with it immediately. Don't walk away, this is called *avoidance*. If you practice avoidance, rest assured that eventually the pent up frustration will spill out, usually at a time or place that has nothing to do with the original situation. In many cases, it will get dumped on someone who had nothing to do with the original issue. Holding frustration and anger inside is a very bad habit. Learning to deal with things immediately will reduce the chances of damaging your interpersonal relationships by misdirecting anger and frustration from work on to those you are close to.

Be willing to walk away from any job if your client is being unreasonable. You want to be fair minded and use common sense, but if you are providing a service or trade to someone who is unwilling to listen to reason, present them with a bill for any outstanding balance and respectfully ask for a check to settle up their account. Thank them for previous work and leave. Do not engage in angry, escalating confrontations with clients. Most likely you are on their property and any negative outcome will affect you more than them. Better to walk away. If they owe you money and refuse to pay, that's what small claims courts are for.

Equipment breaks down, family situations occur, road construction delays happen, as do vehicle accidents. Things aren't always going to run smoothly during a self-employed person's day. Many jobs are set up on a schedule and when unplanned events cause delay, the worst possible response is to become angry and frustrated.

If you will be delayed getting to a job where there is an agreed upon arrival time, immediately call your client and explain the situation. This is an excellent reason to carry a book or electronic device which contains all your clients' phone numbers with you. If your business is dependent on equipment, and it breaks down, the first thing to do is to explain the situation to your current client and then call any other clients scheduled for that day to explain and reschedule if necessary.

Becoming angry only accomplishes negative things: elevated blood pressure, the ability to think clearly (how many times have you done or said things when angry that you later regretted?), loss of clients, jobs and income. Also, there is loss of concentration on the task at hand which can lead to all types of accidents and injuries.

Try practicing something new. Purposefully avoid responding negatively to frustrating things. For instance, the next time an aggressive driver starts to cut you off, here's a novel thought—-slow down and let him in. Most likely you will pass him in traffic later anyway. If someone says something to you that seems designed to get a rise out of you, don't respond. People who do this will eventually stop if they can't get under your skin. If someone insults you publicly, walk away. Once you get the hang of it, you will realize you feel better about yourself for not confronting every person who wants to confront you. Be patient standing in lines—-getting impatient won't make the line move any faster. In fact, you may actually help someone else's day go better by showing patience. If you get to a place through practice where many of life's little annoyances don't negatively affect you, I guarantee you will be a happier and more stress free person. You'll enjoy life more. It may take some work, but it's worth it.

I'm not there yet, but I'm working on it. Practicing patience and positive responses instead of frustration and anger has made me a better person, and a better business owner.

There are some expressions that are timeless. I'm going to close this chapter with one of them. "Do unto others as you would have others do unto you." If we can all learn to live by that principle, the world will be a better place.

Chapter 15
Reality Check

I'VE SPENT A LOT of time extolling the virtues of self-employment. Admittedly, I've focused on the upside. To be fair, there are a number of issues that should be considered and will eventually crop up if you are a self-employed person.

One of the most basic issues is: if you are truly self-employed, then by definition you work by yourself. For many people that's part of the attraction of self-employment. Something to consider is the possibility that if you are seriously injured you won't be able to meet your obligations if your business is one where you have regularly scheduled appointments each week or month. This can also be true if you get sick for more than a few days.

One way to deal with this is to network with someone else in your business and ask for emergency coverage if this should happen. Another solution would be to ask family or friends to cover for you. Any business with a well developed clientele would require more time than most family or friends could supply. Also trusting a competitor to "cover" your jobs while you recuperate might cost you at least some of your clients. Risky, but you may not have a choice.

The best defense is to be careful—both on and off the job. If you choose to be self-employed, you might consider giving up hobbies like mountain climbing, motocross, hang gliding, ultimate fighting and other high risk activities. It would be a shame to build up a clientele over a number of years, then lose most of your clients due to self-inflicted injury in your off work hours that could have been avoided. Of course, you should use maximum caution while performing your work. When lifting, use your legs. I know people get tired of hearing that, but the most common injury that happens to anyone in a physical labor job is back injury.

I have been truly blessed that so far, I have only had one instance serious enough to cause me to miss a day of work. I've tweaked my back, sprained an ankle and cut myself, but managed to limp and gimp through the minor injuries. Still, this is a valid concern when considering a self-employment career. If you are injured or ill, you can't work.

In the five full seasons since I started my own business, here's the scariest health related thing that has happened to me. I'm sharing it to illustrate how easily it could have been avoided. I had a bad habit when I started out. I never ate breakfast and I drank at least a pot of coffee every morning.

One day I got a call for a window cleaning estimate. I drove to the job site, worked up the bid and called the number they'd given me. They wanted the work done immediately. It was about 100 degrees outside, and inside the house the air conditioning had been off a couple of days. We agreed on a price and I started working. About 15 minutes into the job I became dizzy and disoriented. I couldn't figure out what was wrong. Thank goodness I was on the ground and not on the roof! Eventually I was able to call 911 on my cell phone and tell the operator where I was (this process took about 15 minutes) and I was near passing out. I lay on the front porch. That cool concrete was a lifesaver! When the ambulance showed up, they loaded me on a gurney and hauled me to the hospital where I was hooked up to an IV and pumped full of fluids. Within about 20 minutes I was feeling better. They kept me there for an hour and a half of observation before releasing me.

Bottom line, I suffered from heat stroke. No breakfast, coupled with a full pot of coffee had caused me to be dehydrated. Caffeine is a diuretic that pushes water out of your body. Also, I went to the job with no cold drinking water.

The point of sharing this embarrassing moment is that since this incident, I never head out the door to a job without eating a nutritious breakfast and I always carry cold water with me, especially if I'm working in the heat. Drinking water is better than drinking sodas or even "sports drinks" all day. Cool water and if possible filtered water is the healthiest choice you can make. Don't end up in the hospital—or worse—due to poor habits.

Physical fitness and a healthy diet are important. I make no claim to being an expert in either, but I know that someone who stretches every day, works on good cardiovascular health and who eats a diet that includes healthy doses of fresh fruits, vegetables and whole grains will over time feel better and be healthier. They will also be less vulnerable to injury. Eating a balanced diet and exercising regularly will also help your body fight off infections and common illnesses like colds and flu. You may still get 'em, but if you eat well and are in good shape, your body will be much better prepared to fight them off.

Here's another thing people probably get tired of hearing. During cold and flu season (really, all the time) the best and easiest thing you can do to avoid becoming ill is to regularly wash your hands. Consistently washing and disinfecting your hands can potentially save you downtime in your business due to being sick. Regular hand washing is the simplest health tip I can give you. I carry a bottle of rubbing alcohol in my truck for use as a disinfectant after most public outings. Door handles, pens in banks, counter tops, gasoline pump handles, after shaking hands—-these are all good times to disinfect, especially during cold and flu season.

I've touched on the idea that when you own your own business you are the boss. That's true in every aspect. You are the CEO, accountant, negotiator, bill collector and worker. Each of these areas requires different skills and most people have, at least, some learning to do. A person may be a great worker, but not have well developed people skills. Another person may have a great business idea and the money to make it happen, but absolutely no work skills. The point is, when you own a business you will need to learn all aspects of being the boss. This is a good thing and will benefit you the rest of your life whether you stay self-employed or eventually go back to being an employee.

Most small business owners are frugal. When you are responsible for all the expenses involved not only in maintaining your home life but also those related to running your business, you will soon realize that wasting money is unacceptable. Each dollar is hard earned and vital to the continued success of your business as well as your non-working life.

Maintaining a monthly budget is important because as your business grows, you need to know if your expenses are also growing. Unless you know what your expenses are, you won't know how much profit your efforts are producing. Trust me here, this is important. Come tax time, you need to know and be able to document each and every expense incurred in your business. Since you write them off against your earnings, every legitimate expense you claim is money in your pocket. Keeping a monthly budget will make tax time infinitely less of a hassle.

That's a great lead-in to the subject of taxes. As employees, many people can get away with filing the 1040 EZ form. Payroll taxes are automatically deducted by their employer and they can (especially if they rent their living quarters) file a single sheet of paper at tax time. If they own a home, they will probably want to file the regular 1040 form to take mortgage related exemptions.

As a small business owner, you WILL be filing the long form. In addition, there are many other forms you will want to file. These have to do with depreciating your equipment costs over time, including the primary vehicle you use for your business and, depending on what your business entails, many other pieces of equipment. As I stated in an earlier chapter, unless you want to add tax expert to the list of things you must learn, I heartily recommend hiring an *accredited* accountant. That means they went to school and have a degree in accounting.

At tax time there are a lot of people who hang out a sign and charge people money to fill out tax forms. If you use someone like this, make sure it is someone you trust. They will have access to your personal financial information. Also, they may not be able to help you if you are audited. Most certified accountants will, for a fee, either take care of the audit for you or go to the audit with you.

I got myself in tax trouble when I started out. I can only blame myself since my first accountant told me to set aside money for self-employment taxes (30 percent) and I just didn't listen. I treated having an accountant as a "magic wand" that would make the tax issue go away. Three years later, I am finally getting close to paying off the debt caused by that mistake.

If this book saves even one person from making the mistakes I made by not setting aside the proper amount of Self Employment Tax in the manner required by the IRS, it will have been worth all the work of writing and revising that went into its creation. Nothing has caused me more stress than being in hot water with the IRS. It is to be avoided at all costs!

Regular equipment maintenance is a must in self-employment, including oil and filter changes in your business vehicle, as well as regular tire rotation and new tires when needed. That vehicle is your business. If it's not in good running order, you can't get to your jobs.

Next in line is whatever equipment you use to perform your work. Regular maintenance will make any machine work better and last longer. From my experience, it's better to buy the absolute best equipment you can afford, rather than trying to save money by buying cheap equipment. If you spend the money up front and buy commercial grade, top-end machines and perform regular maintenance, odds are they will last longer than two or three cheap machines.

You will have to learn to have a phone that's on 24/7. Hopefully, most people will call at reasonable hours, but that phone is how you make money. You want people to be able to make contact with you easily, leave messages if you are unavailable and you definitely want to be checking for messages at every possible opportunity. If it rings late at night or early in the morning, it's a small price to pay in order to have a successful business.

You will have days where you want to pull out your hair and find yourself screaming at the sky, "Why did I become self-employed! I HATE THIS!" Once you calm down and start thinking rationally again, you will realize that you had incidents similar to this when you worked for an employer. There, you could blame co-workers or the company or your supervisor or manager. When you are self-employed you can only blame yourself or your client.

In my experience, most of the times I've ended up having a meltdown hasn't been my client's fault. Remember the chapter on dealing with frustration? The things I included in that chapter aren't cute little sayings I pulled out of someone else's self-help book. Those things are hard earned wisdom gleaned from dealing with issues and situations in my own life and businesses. Be prepared to deal with anything! As a business owner, if it has to be dealt with, it's up to you.

Chapter 16
Recession

As I FOUND OUT during 2007, there are times when the tried and true methods of advertising don't produce the normal 1 percent return. One of those times is when the country is in a recession. The big financial crisis hit in 2008, but I think working people were noticing and reacting to large price increases in everyday items and pulling back on their discretionary spending as early as March of 2007. Grocery items, clothing and fuel costs were starting to skyrocket—especially fuel. In fact, many of the price increases were due to the high cost of fuel. Transporting all the things we use every day takes trucks, ships, trains and planes. All of them use one type of fuel or another. Those costs get passed on to you and me.

I walked 1,200 fliers during March of 2007 and received one call for a lawn estimate. That's less than one-tenth of 1 percent. Guess my price was too high because I didn't get that job. During that time I did pick up a job from the magnetic signs on my truck. (Good plug for magnetic vehicle signs.)

You can still grow a small business during a recession, but you have to work hard and smart. Since most types of advertising boil down to a numbers game (the more ads you put out, the more responses you are likely to get) you will need to double, if not triple, your advertising during a recession. Also, it's a really good idea to focus your efforts in affluent neighborhoods. If folks can afford to live in a really expensive home and drive a really expensive vehicle, they can probably afford to hire out some services—even in tough times. Basically, by focusing on more affluent neighborhoods, you are playing the odds.

During an economic recession, be flexible. If necessary to make ends meet be willing to take on a part time job. Even if you are self-employed, keep in touch with people you know who have businesses or work in businesses that need temporary labor (especially if the person happens to be in the personnel department!) Periodically ask them how business is for their company.

Recessions are a great reason to build a savings account. Nothing will help you through tough economic times more than a few thousand dollars sitting in a savings account at your local bank. I can hear many of you thinking, "There's no way I can save a few thousand dollars. I don't have $100 saved and I need every penny I have just to get by!"

I started a savings account this year for the first time, and have made a practice of putting at least 5 percent of my gross monthly income in there before I pay my bills. In fact, I've been averaging more like 7–8 percent. For me, that means a reserve of about $1,700. If I don't need it for taxes this year, I'll be able to at least double that by the end of next year.

My experience in building a savings account is a road map for you. Go to a local bank and open a passbook savings account. Determine to put a set amount or a certain percentage in every month, no matter what. Instead of saying to yourself, "I just can't do it—-tell yourself I have to do it." Make it a priority. You'll thank me later.

It may take two or three years to build it up, but when the next recession hits (and it will) you won't be caught unprepared. That money will provide a safety net for you and your family. Resist the temptation to use even a penny of it for anything other than a true emergency. You may not earn much interest on the money, but it will be easily accessible should you ever need it.

Recessions are a tough time for everyone. As the economy tanks, most people pull back on spending. That hurts manufacturers, retailers and service providers. Most of the small businesses envisioned in this book would fall into the service provider category.

Be flexible. If your work has a seasonal nature, there's nothing wrong with working for someone else during your off season. In fact, you will be able to build your wealth much faster if you do work, rather than sitting around vegetating for four or five months and using up your savings on living expenses.

In good financial times or bad, make a plan for bad times. Be prepared. The key to surviving in tough times is having a strategy in place when bad times hit and sticking to it for the duration of the economic downturn. Once things start getting better, make it a priority to replace any reserves that were used surviving the recession ASAP. Being financially prepared is a lifetime priority. Saving money seems to be a lost art in America. Start a new tradition in your own life and the life of your family. Be savers. A day may come where those savings make all the difference for your business and your family.

Chapter 17
Beyond Self Employment

IT'S NEVER TOO SOON to think beyond personal physical labor work. Regardless of the type of service you choose, there is always the option of hiring employees to do the actual work while you manage the overall business and seek new accounts. Of course, that brings into play all the different issues involved in managing people. Some folks are up for it and some aren't.

It is very difficult for employees and self-employed people to become wealthy from their work efforts. Employees are always limited by the wage their employer is willing to pay them and self-employed people are limited by the number of hours in a day. When you are trading hours for dollars, there is a limit to how much you can earn. In many self-employment occupations that limit can be much higher than what companies will pay in wages, but it is still limited.

If you know that hiring and dealing with employees is not in your future, start thinking about what other types of things you can do to create new income streams in addition to your current service or trade. You never know—one of your ideas could eventually replace your service work.

Here's a challenge. Instead of four hours of television every evening take a day off from the tube, get a pad and pen and start writing down ideas for new business ventures. Just brainstorm— nothing is too far out there. Write 'em down. Once you have a list, do more critical thinking about each idea. Is it feasible? What tools or equipment do you need? How much time does it require? Will you have to travel to do it? Doing this, once a month, may help you find your next business venture. That's worth giving up a night of watching television. Every minute I watch television is a minute I'm not thinking.

What experience do you have in life? Is there something you are an expert in that is totally different than what you currently do to make money? One option is to write a book like I've done and share that information with people. Another option is to put together a training seminar on your area of expertise and market it to corporations, organizations, groups or individuals. Are you artistic? Teach people how to paint or sculpt or blow glass or whatever it is you do.

If you are a collector of antiques or memorabilia, build up your collection, then consider setting aside some of the finds you make for resale. If you have duplicate items, or just find a good price on things you know will be profitable but aren't good enough for your collection, buy them and resell them for profit.

Observe the world around you. What things do people either not have the ability to do or just don't want to do for themselves? Can you offer a service doing that for more money than you are making now, with less physical labor?

Another area of concern in self-employment is looking toward retirement. Every single day all of us are getting older and, at some point, aren't going to want to be providing physical labor services or trades to folks. Planning for retirement is your responsibility.

There are many tried and true methods that would include, but are not limited to, owning investment properties and rentals, investing in stocks/bonds/certificates of deposit, commodities, precious metals or collecting valuable objects.

One of the best long term investments most of us can make is buying our own home. If you are currently renting, you are making the owner of that property wealthy. Every time you pay rent, the owner uses your money to pay off his mortgage. Good deal for him, bad financial deal for you.

Purchasing your own home is the one investment I feel very comfortable in recommending. I have owned two different homes now and in both cases the value of the properties increased over the time I owned them. Also, each time I make a mortgage payment I reduce the outstanding debt which adds to the equity I have in the property. If you choose a home in a decent neighborhood with a mortgage payment you can comfortably afford the chances are you will make money over time on your investment. If you have been watching the news recently, there are a lot of people in danger of losing their homes because they got talked into a mortgage payment higher than they could comfortably afford. There's a lesson in that for all of us. The safest mortgage you can get to finance your home is a fixed mortgage. The most common one is a thirty year fixed mortgage.

If you have some past credit issues that lenders tell you will disqualify you from a fixed rate mortgage, instead of jumping at a riskier type of loan like an Adjustable Rate Mortgage (ARM), start a process of repairing your credit rating. The first step here is to obtain a copy of your credit history. It will show all the past issues that are keeping your credit score low. Start calling each creditor and resolve the issues they have with you. Once you and they agree that you have satisfied them, ask them to contact the credit services in writing and request that the incident be removed from your credit history. After a couple of months, you should call the credit services to see if the individual creditor followed through.

I'm not saying this will be easy. It may take a year or two. Don't take the easy way of borrowing a large amount of money through a risky loan. Take the time and build your credit rating to a point where you can qualify for a more secure fixed rate loan. Your home ownership will be safer and having a solid credit rating only helps you in every financial area of life, including business.

Honestly, owning my own home has created more wealth for me than any other investment I've ever made. In terms of planning for your future, I don't think there's a better place you can park some of your money than in your own house.

America is different than most other countries in the world. The underlying financial principle in our country is *capitalism*. What that means is that anyone who has an idea and is willing to work hard to make that idea a reality (within the boundaries set by the law) can realize their dream. If you want to be a housekeeper in America, you learn how to do the job, get business cards, find clients and you are a professional housekeeper. In many socialist countries, there are layers of bureaucracy you must negotiate to get a permit or license to do that work. The process can take months or years!

I know someone who came to the U.S. from another country. Once, during a conversation they stated that in their opinion their country was superior to America in many educational and social aspects. I listened for awhile, then asked this question. "Well, if your country is so much better than America, why aren't you there?" The response says it all—"Oh, well there's just so much more opportunity here!"

If you have a dream, you are free to pursue it. If working in a factory for $8 per hour isn't your dream, consider doing something else. What is your dream? Do you have one? If not, why not? I'm not advocating quitting a job that is meeting your financial needs. I am suggesting that you can use your current job as a springboard to something else. Certainly, there's no reason you can't look into other possibilities while you continue your current employment.

I am thankful for every job I have had in my life. I am especially thankful for the opportunity to experience self-employment. There's just nothing like knowing you went out with your God given talents and built up your own enterprise and are making a living from it. Nothing else comes close—at least that's my experience.

Chapter 18
Random Thoughts and Observations

ONE OF THE THINGS I've discovered during the forty-nine years I've lived is how important it is to be able to laugh at myself and at life. People who are ultra serious about everything miss out on so much life has to offer. The old expression that "laughter is the best medicine" has a basis in fact. I'm much mellower now that I ever was during my fourteen years in the electronics industry. I hope that someday I will get to a place where it is impossible to make me angry. If I can arrive at that place, I will have accomplished something.

Always be willing to learn new things from anyone who can teach you. I'm not saying to believe whatever someone tells you, but be willing to look at their advice or their philosophy objectively. One thing people can do in life is to learn how to research any given subject. With the advent of the internet and search engines, any subject can be researched easily. Every person on earth has a story and knowledge. Not everyone has the same story or knowledge, so I can learn from literally everyone I meet if I'm willing to listen. Being a good listener is an extremely valuable tool.

There's an expression that's been around for a few years, "Think outside the box." It's been used a lot in advertising campaigns and in corporate America. I would encourage you to embrace the concept as you continue on in life.

I wrote this book because I read a free e-book that suggested it. After reading that suggestion I thought, "Why not? I've been self-employed for six years and can share a lot of what I've learned and a lot of good advice that was passed on to me by my brother Bobby. Writing a book was definitely outside the box for me. When I was in school, English classes were my favorites. I'd just never considered the possibility of writing for publication. Not until the suggestion that maybe I could, came to me through the writings of a total stranger. Thinking outside your own personal "box" could be the key to your future financial freedom.

There are two qualities that will make anyone successful in life if they are practiced faithfully.

1) Don't be afraid to try something new.
2) If it fails don't be afraid to get back up, start over and try again.

Many millionaires have made and lost more than one fortune because they understood those two qualities. Failure is an opportunity to learn what doesn't work. Trying again and again are opportunities to succeed.

Go through life asking questions and being observant. A guy noticed one day how aggressively cheat grass managed to stick and hold in his socks. He was a scientist so he asked himself how it did that, and then he thought about how to create the same effect with man made materials. The end result was the product we call Velcro. If that guy was smart he patented the idea and is living on an island somewhere sipping cold drinks on the beach. How many things have you used in your life that had Velcro on them?

Anyone can have an idea no one has thought of before. You can have that idea. If you think you have an original idea, be very careful who you tell or show it to. Practice some research skills and look into the patent process. You might be the next person to be sitting on an island drinking cold beverages and watching the waves roll in on the beach!

The human body isn't designed to work seven days in a row. Make it a practice to take at least one day off every week. If you are a church going person, since you are already worshipping that day anyway, why not just shut down the business for the whole day. If you aren't a church going person, choose a day that you will be away from your business. You decide when and when not to work. Make your work schedule conform to your life. Taking a day off each week will also help you stay healthy. Getting enough sleep on a daily basis and having a day of rest each week will help you be better prepared to deal with your business.

Make it a point, when you get into conversations with new people, to work in the fact that you are self-employed. Toot your own horn! If you do a number of different things, make sure they know all of them. It's amazing how many times during conversations, once people heard I provided this or that service, they immediately asked me for an estimate. Bobby's right, don't be a secret agent. Tell everyone who you are and what you do!

Here's something it took me a lot of years to figure out. Life is short. Learn to enjoy your family, your friends, your clients and even the strangers you meet. Most of all, learn to enjoy yourself.

In closing this book, I want to encourage everyone who has a dream of owning their own small business to take steps to make it a reality. If you have a great idea and never do anything with it, it's just an idea. Taking that idea out of your brain and putting it on paper is the first step to making it real. Printing business cards is the second step to making it real. Distributing the business cards or fliers to potential clients is the third step. When the first call comes in and someone hires you to provide your service or trade and you get that first check, it's not an idea anymore. It IS real. Your idea has become your business.

Congratulations and good luck!

LaVergne, TN USA
21 April 2010
180066LV00004B/178/P